MW00942224

RESOLVE, COURAGE, HOPE

Resolve, Courage, Hope

Scott Headley & Alison Nissen

Copyright © 2016 by Scott Headley & Alison Nissen.

Library of Congress Control Number:		2016906336
ISBN:	Hardcover	978-1-5144-8601-6
	Softcover	978-1-5144-8600-9
	eBook	978-1-5144-8599-6

All rights reserved. No part of this book may be reproduced or transmitted in any form or by any means, electronic or mechanical, including photocopying, recording, or by any information storage and retrieval system, without permission in writing from the copyright owner.

Any people depicted in stock imagery provided by Thinkstock are models, and such images are being used for illustrative purposes only. Certain stock imagery © Thinkstock.

Print information available on the last page.

Rev. date: 05/03/2016

To order additional copies of this book, contact:
Xlibris
1-888-795-4274
www.Xlibris.com
Orders@Xlibris.com
737165

Alison,

There are no words that adequately describe the deep gratitude I have for you. I am convinced God set our paths on a collision course knowing you were the perfect person to help me with this book. I appreciate the patience and empathy you gave during this heart wrenching project.

This book played a necessary part in my emotional recovery. Thanks to you, the words made it from my heart and mind to paper and will help others in difficult situations find hope.

Sincerely,
Scott Headley

For Mom, my cheerleader, my mentor, my friend.

--Alison

CONTENTS

The following is a memoir of Scott's recollections and interpretations of events. I have researched news-related sources and court documents to assemble the facts as they are known to the general public. Some names have been changed, dialogue recreated, and timelines altered.

Alison Nissen

Just a Moment
and a Drink

I just needed a moment and a drink. I sat on the barstool and flagged the bartender. I'd been there before; he knew what to pour. I wrapped my hands around the glass, and I pulled a long, slow sip. It went down easy and smooth. I breathed in and relaxed my shoulders, closed my eyes, and blocked out the din of the restaurant. This was my private time.

Maybe I should have been home with my wife eating dinner or watching the game with friends. Maybe, but I wasn't. I was sitting at a bar in a small town twenty-five miles from home, cupping my drink, and breathing in the lingering smell of fried food.

I hadn't had a full night's sleep in almost a year. My days were spent rebuilding an office and running a business; my nights were spent saving the world—not literally saving the world, but protecting the ones I loved from fires or robberies or bad men with guns. Going home after work meant going to sleep, and going to sleep meant nightmares. So I stalled, sat at a bar, and ordered a drink.

The bar was centered just inside the front door. On a slow day, a half-dozen people will spread around the heavily shellacked rectangular structure while diners eat at the tables to the left and right. Today was a slow, dark, drizzly day. I sat and drank and blocked out the hushed sounds of patrons. Or maybe I blocked out the memories.

I ordered my second drink, glad for a barkeep who knew how to mind his business. A man set his phone on the bar next to me and smiled. "Hey, you're Scott Headley, right?"

He stood about six feet, dressed in a parka with some logo on it. He held his hand out for me to shake. I wasn't on my best behavior. I nodded.

"Scott, I've just got to ask you about what happened."

I've been asked this question ten thousand times.

"My wife and I, we're clients at the Lake Wales office. My wife, she was really shaken up. After the incident, she couldn't stop talking about how sweet and nice those women were. You've just got to tell me."

"I'm sorry, it's not something I talk about." I smiled, or tried to smile, and shook my head.

"Please, Scott, it would mean the world to me. I know my wife has been so concerned."

"You know . . ." I paused. I didn't recall his name.

"Jake—Jake and Brenda Johnson."

"Jake, I'm sorry," I mumbled in a soft, polite tone. "I just came here for a drink and a moment."

"Just a few minutes, Scott."

"Jake." I didn't continue my thought. I raised the glass up to my lips and pulled another sip.

"Sure, sure, you have your moment."

I sighed, audibly relieved. Jake Johnson retreated to a table on the other side of the bar where he could discuss the weather or the kids or local politics with his female companion.

Lake Wales is a small rural town in Central Florida. Surrounded by lakes and farms, it is home to an orange juicing plant, about fourteen thousand people, and my small field office. I own and manage an insurance company. My employees are handpicked by me. Most start at the bottom and work their way up. A year ago, two of my shining stars died because of a fire that started in my office.

Ever since then, I've fought to keep everybody I know safe. I closed my eyes and blocked the memory. I drained the last sip of my glass and gently set it on the bar, listening to the sound of the ice as it rattled against the tumbler.

"Scott." Jake Johnson appeared at my side.

Startled, I looked up.

"Scott, you've had your moment. You've got to tell me what happened."

Why not, I thought, the alcohol limited my sensibilities. "Okay, are you sitting with your wife?" I pointed to his table.

He nodded.

"Great, just let me settle up, and I'll meet you over there."

A few minutes later, I pulled out the chair between them. Brenda smiled at me, her face fresh and open—no cares in the world. But I expected she would be the one who needed a drink and a moment shortly.

DECEMBER 13, 2007

At 3:45 p.m., my phone pinged. "Scott, are you alone?" the caller asked.

"I'm traveling by myself. My wife's at home." I answered, glancing at my gas gauge, which read full. It was not unusual for me to travel between our three offices by myself. I'd stop at the main office in Lakeland, meet a few clients, run some numbers, and check on accounts. I'd travel to the other two offices later in the day to assist the sales team or office managers if they needed guidance.

"I don't want you to panic."

On December 13, my wife drove me home after my morning visit to the main office. I wasn't feeling well and needed a nap. Instead, I'd received a worrisome phone call about the office in Lake Wales. A customer had called a handful of minutes earlier. The office doors were locked, an odd event for midday. Normally, there were three people staffing the small, main-street office. The business is to stay open during normal hours, and it is company policy to never allow only one employee to man the office by themselves. This particular week, one of the employees was on a pre-Christmas vacation. Two was the rule. I hopped in the car, leaving my wife without a ride.

"Okay," I tried to reassure the voice on the other end of the phone I wouldn't panic. When the initial call came in regarding the locked doors, an agent at the main office in Lakeland called a business in Lake Wales, which sat across the street from our building, to see if everything seemed okay. Rather than wait at home for the response, I started to drive. The traffic, light; my heart beating heavy. Alone on a four-lane suburban street, I slowly began to panic.

"There's a fire at the office."

I looked down the road. Spanish moss draped over oak trees created playful shadows on the road. "Is anyone hurt?"

"The girls." I gripped the steering wheel. My truck speed shifted from forty-five miles per hour to seventy. Ivanna, the twenty-six-year-old office manager, and Julieta, the twenty-year-old salesclerk, felt more like family than employees.

"But I don't think he burnt them. I think it was the gasoline."

My fingers turned white. The truck speed rose to eighty-five.

"For the robbery," the voice continued.

I pushed the gas pedal to the floorboard. The back end of the truck fishtailed, spraying bits of gravel across the street. If there was a red light, I didn't stop. I just begged the truck to move faster.

Rounding the corner, I saw a sheriff's cruiser across a divided highway with a stopped motorist. The truck gunned through three lanes of traffic as if on autopilot. I locked my brakes. The tires skidded from the road to the median; bits of mud and rock were tossed into the air. I jumped out; the smell of rubber on asphalt and fresh-cut grass filled the air.

"I need everybody you can get me in Lake Wales."

"Sir, Lake Wales is not my jurisdiction. That's twenty miles away."

"I need you," I enunciated each word slowly, "to send everybody you can to my office in Lake Wales."

The officer rolled his eyes up from his ticket book. He had just witnessed a madman cross a busy street, tear up the grass, and shout orders. I wondered if he could hear the panic in my voice.

I continued my tirade. "My employees are hurt. Now!"

"You need to tell me what's going on," he finally said; he was beginning to look overwhelmed with my insistency.

"I don't have time to explain it to you. There's my tag number." I pointed. "I'm not stopping until I get to Lake Wales."

Jumping back in my truck, I ripped through the median, lit the road up with my tires, and left additional tread marks in my wake. I wanted him to pursue me. If I were being chased, the lights would get me to where I needed to go. He didn't bite. My speedometer went higher.

One of the greatest attributes of our business is that we are family. On occasion, I've even been asked if Ivanna Barrera and Julieta Lovato were my daughters. They spoke the language of best friends. I recruited Ivanna six years ago at the age of twenty. A mother of two, she lived with her fiancé in a nearby neighborhood. Her gregarious personality endeared her to customers and coworkers alike. She had a knack for remembering names and making clients feel at home.

Ivanna recruited her sister-in-law, Julieta, who also lived in Lake Wales and was excited to be expecting her third child, a boy, in three months. Julieta was shy and private, sweet and gentle. Clients gravitated to her kind disposition. They worked well together—always helpful, always cheerful. I was proud to have them as employees.

I picked up my phone again and dialed.

"911. Please state your emergency."

"This is Scott Headley, my employees have been burnt. My office has been robbed," I talked fast.

"Mr. Headley," the operator spoke steadily. "I need you to calm down. Can you give me the address?"

"The Nationwide Insurance office at 124 West Central Avenue in Lake Wales." There was a tightening in my stomach, a knot caused by alarm and fear.

"Mr. Headley, we already have emergency vehicles at that location. Sir, can you tell me where you are?"

"I'm going there now." My tire suspension scraped a set of railroad tracks.

"Mr. Headley, are you driving?" the dispatcher asked.

"Yes, I'm driving."

"I need to ask you to be careful. An accident would only complicate the situation."

"Then quit distracting me." I glanced at the speedometer, which read 91 mph. I slammed shut my phone and threw it onto the seat beside me. It bounced, and my lifeline jittered to a stop on the rubberized floor.

Arriving in Lake Wales in less than half the normal time, I rammed my truck into a parking lot about half a block from the office. Yellow tape had been draped across the avenue, preventing me from entering the lot behind our building; beyond the tape, steam rose from the office roof. Lake Wales police cruisers, ambulances, and fire trucks were parked helter-skelter around the street.

I hopped out of the truck, slammed the door, and desperately ran toward the building. My breath arduous as I took giant steps over the curb toward the front door; my voice hoarse as it repeatedly called out, "Ivanna! Julieta!"

A handful of reporters stood around the perimeter and started shoving cameras in my face. Surprised by their attention, I glanced at my company shirt, embroidered Headley Insurance in plain block letters.

Herbert Gillis, the Lake Wales chief of police, motioned for me to come under the tape. "You, in the Headley shirt, do you work here?"

I nodded. The smoke, thick and heavy, caught in my throat. "I'm Scott Headley," I rasped, a cough rolling off my tongue.

"I need everything you can get me on a guy named Leon Davis. Stay here," he demanded, "in case I want any other information."

Pushing my sunglasses to the top of my head, I moved next to the fire truck. Flipping open my cell, I called the main office, repeating the chief's orders, grateful for the phone in my hand. "I need everything you've got on this guy—social, birthday, address."

I'd been in Lake Wales for no more than one minute; adrenaline coursed through my body. I closed my phone; another police officer grabbed my collar and pushed me toward the reporters. I dug my shoes into the pavement, refusing to budge.

"Get off me!" I shouted and wiped the spittle from my mouth. On an ordinary day, I would not challenge authority, but on December 13, 2007, nothing was ordinary.

"You're in the middle of a crime scene. You can't be here."

I leaned in and bowed up before swiping at his hand on my shirt. "My employees are in there!"

He held on and pulled me closer; he was now close enough to me that I could smell his stale breath. "Your employees aren't here. Stay outside the tape," he ordered; his intensity matched mine.

"Lieutenant, Scott," Chief Gillis said. He stepped in between us and pointed toward the sky, his firm tone defusing the situation. "The women are on their way to the hospital."

Clenching my phone, I looked up. Police and news helicopters circled above like vultures. I suddenly heard the cacophony of harsh chopping discord vibrating off the surrounding buildings. Realizing my employees—my girls—my sweet, thoughtful, kind friends were in a life-flight helicopter, my stomach turned. I looked down at the phone in my hand and held it tighter.

Ivanna and Julieta, lovers of life and family and good things, they knew everyone in town, and I bet they could tell me about the emergency personnel who were putting out the fire and the onlookers who had come to watch. I stood motionless. I wanted to roll up my sleeves to help, to protect them.

Forced to stand behind the tape, I felt powerless. The photographers continued to click away, but all I could do was look at the phone in my hand—my connection to the outside world, a world where things were normal. However, other than the twinkling Christmas tree mocking me in the front window of the office, nothing was normal. I had driven recklessly, watched my building smolder, and worried like hell for my employees. At that moment, Ivanna and Julieta were swiftly being carried to the Orlando Regional Medical Center.

*   *   *

At the same time I stood outside the building, the police told the local businesses to lock their doors while an active manhunt ensued. Leon Davis Jr., the man in question, had been a Headley Insurance customer for years. I was told he knew the women well; he lived in the same community. He played pickup basketball with the girls' fiancés. Ivanna even dated his brother in high school.

At approximately three thirty that afternoon, Davis quietly walked into the office carrying a gun, a container of gasoline, duct tape, and a lighter. While Ivanna and Julieta were busy filing, he locked the front door, placed tape over the surveillance cameras, and at gun point, demanded they open the safe. Next, he escorted them into the bathroom where he secured them by taping their hands together and wrapping their heads with more tape to prevent them from screaming. He doused them with gasoline and flicked the lighter. Before leaving, he poured the remaining gasoline around the office. He lit it all on fire. At three thirty-nine, a silent alarm warned the local fire department.

At 3:39, Erin Addleson, a Headley customer, tried to enter the front door to pay her bill. She paused and called the Lakeland office then tried the door again. Davis unlocked the door from the inside and told her the building was on fire.

At 3:39, Ivanna and Julieta ran out the back door screaming, their shoes burned off, their clothes and hair bright with embers. The fire had melted the tape and allowed them to escape—Ivanna ran toward the front of the building, and Julieta hobbled across the street to the Havana Nights restaurant. Davis, hearing the girls' screams, circled back to follow them.

At 3:39, Gabriel Brooks and his family decided to investigate the sudden plume of smoke rising above the building one street over. Lake Wales is the type of town where businesses and residents live and work together. Heading to the back of the Headley Building, Brooks heard screams and ran to offer assistance. Seeing Julieta still on fire, he began to put the flames out with his hands. Looking up, he noticed Davis in determined pursuit. Brooks watched Davis pull a gun from an orange lunch container and shoot. In that split second, Brooks turned his head. His children and wife, who trailed behind, began to scream. He watched his wife put her hands to her face. He mimicked her motion then dropped to the ground. A bullet had passed through the side of his nose.

At 3:39, Farah Moody, another neighbor, came to inspect the commotion. She ducked behind a small chain-link fence. She witnessed Brooks fall to the ground. She watched Davis place his gun back into the orange lunch container and calmly walk away. Ripping off her T-shirt, she gave it to Brooks to use as a bandage then rushed toward Ivanna.

At 3:39, while fleeing across the street, Julieta bumped into a passing car. The driver parked and helped Julieta into the restaurant. There, Julieta sat, naked, with burnt tape around her hands and neck. She laid a menu over her protruding belly and prayed for her baby's life. The driver noted a sedan, which had been parked in front of the restaurant, was gone.

Ivanna continued walking around the Headley building. Seeing Addleson's car, she rested against the large SUV while she waited for help to arrive. Moody stepped forward and offered assistance. Ivanna screamed and cried that she was hot. Much of her skin was charred or brilliant red; her skirt, black nylon, was melted to her; and her shirt was gone. Moody ran to the restaurant across the street and asked for ice water. When she returned, Moody held the cup while Ivanna took small, shallow sips. Ivanna repeatedly asked Moody why someone would rob her; she didn't have any money. "Pray for my kids. Pray for me, Farah," Ivanna said. "I don't think I'm going to make it."[1]

*　　*　　*

I stood outside the yellow tape and lit a cigarette, a nervous habit that calmed my nerves. I looked at my phone and waited for a call from the other office. My battery light flashed. In front of the stone-faced, single-story building leaned an adjustable ladder. Two fire fighters stood on top of the roof—one holding a chainsaw and the other, a long metal rod. I was overcome with the acidic smell of burnt plastic and wood. Bile rose from my stomach, and I dropped to my knees to vomit.

I stayed on all fours, helpless, while a crowd began to gather. No longer noticing the helicopters, I felt the eyes of every small-town and big-city reporter. I imagined the heat of their bodies engulfing me. Emotionally wrought and embarrassed, I huddled on my hands and knees on a gravely asphalt parking lot. From my lowly position, a set of men's shoes were visible behind me, blocking me from the reporters' intrusiveness. The man slowly got down on the ground and put his arm around my back.

He was a stranger to me, but he called me by name. "Hey, Scott," he said, "I've got your back." Bill Bair introduced himself. At that moment, however, he was more than just an onlooker; he was my savior from the swarm of spectators invading my turf.

I finally stood, dizzy and unbalanced. A woman with a friendly hug gathered me into her arms. "Baby, do you have anyone here with you?" I recognized her as someone I should know, a customer—maybe. A local shop owner—maybe. I shook my head no. "Well, I'm going to get you some help. You don't need to be all alone." And then she was gone from both my sight and my memory.

The scene continued to evolve. I was no longer aware of the building. Chief Gillis filled me in on some details. As our conversation waned, he leaned in and quietly said, "Scott, this case seems oddly familiar to another case. You know what's going on in Lake Alfred?"

I stared at him. Lake Alfred, a community only a few miles away, had been in the news all week—a man in a baggy sweatshirt, his head covered, tried to rob a closed BP station. He couldn't get in. In frustration, he shot two clerks who were changing the store sign. He killed them execution-style. Video showed he drove away in a sedan. An impassioned plea and an offer of a substantial reward for information had been announced. My stomach turned again.

In the confusion, I saw a second friendly face—my contractor, who happened to be on his way to the office to do some repair work. He was older, probably seventy, and a real gruff, to-the-point type of guy. I heard him ask in disbelief, "He did what to them girls?" Someone told him, and he replied, "Ain't that just a hair in a nose." Tears welled in his gentle eyes, but they never made it past the surface. He was the last guy I'd ever expect to cry.

My cell rang, the vibration jolting me from my agony. "Do you need me to come?" a voice asked.

"Yes," I replied.

After that, someone else called, asking the same question. I gave the same answer, unsure of how my voice managed to respond when I only had the strength to nod.

Slowly, the entire Headley Insurance Agency arrived. My team, which included my children, stood with me, prayed with me, worried with me. Imagining the burns Ivanna and Julieta felt, I asked for water, not for myself, but for my employees who suffered in a hospital fifty-three miles away. I asked for so many bottles that, in the morning, thirty half-empty bottles ended up the floorboard of my truck.

I remember only snatches of the day—like a grisly photo scrapbook. Click—a large crowd of rubberneckers gathered around the yellow crime scene tape. Click—a woman behind me pointing to the sawed-off roof. "That's how he escaped!" Click—dry-heaving in the parking lot. Click—praying on the cold bathroom floor of the car wash nearby.

I'm told I drove home that night. I don't recall. Family members and a few friends came over to the house later. We stood on the back porch and prayed some more. The Lake Wales police department gave the all clear at 10:30 p.m. "Come secure your building," they said. I tried to go, but some of my favorite people wouldn't let me. Ben Mitchell—my friend, former employee, and cousin-in-law, along with my seventeen-year-old son, Josh, went instead. It didn't matter that it was late at night. I'd already had my last good night of sleep.

THE IMMEDIATE AFTERMATH

Eighteen stressful hours after the fire, I arrived at the Lake Wales office. The blue Nationwide Insurance & Financial Services sign hung on the building facade unscathed. The picture window, inches to the right, had cracked and fallen away. Bits of glass clung to the frame and littered the sidewalk outside. Plastic vertical blinds, withered and twisted into thin ribbons, waved gently in the breeze.

I entered the building, crunching over glass and debris. I choked on the stench of burnt hair mixed with scorched meat and campfire ash. A metallic smell that tasted like copper made my eyes water. And all the melted plastic—it was a sticky smell that clung to the air like a fine mist.

Josh and Ben ran interference. Arriving on the scene shortly after the all clear the night before, they had secured the building to protect it from looters. They couldn't do much in the middle of the night but pick through pieces of ash and rubble and keep vandals away. They tried to begin a rudimentary cleanup, but how does someone clean up such a horrific event? How does someone hide the pungent scent of charred plaster and melted carpeting?

The fire left etched, jagged lines at its border. Below the yellowed edge, the texture thickened to char and layered like bark. The damage to the office was extensive, yet the copier looked salvageable. The floor covering had blackened and warped, yet the angel atop the Christmas tree smiled at me. My hands began to tremble.

I am the patriarch of my family and business, the protector, the one who teaches and encourages and guides. My son looked at me. His youthful eyes, no longer innocent, had seen the grotesque remnants of terror. "Dad," he said. His teenage voice cracked as he tried to comfort me. "I'm so sorry."

Nothing could have prepared me for what I saw. The once-vibrant office, decorated with flowers and photographs and drawings from children, was in shambles. Workstations, abandoned, lay in ruins and covered with bits of fallen ceiling tiles.

Studying the scene, I envisioned the horror that Ivanna and Julieta had faced. Pieces of the bathroom door lay catawampus across the floor. The women escaped by breaking it down. I stepped around and walked into the bathroom.

Next to the sink, a bloody footprint—Julieta's. Her shoes had been taken into custody. Next to the door, a right footprint. I placed my feet next to each print and walked her tortured path. Strips of clothing had singed and melted and dropped on the ground in intervals. The steps led to the back door. My hands mimicked the fingerprints that were left on the handle. A fingernail stuck to the edge. I continued out the door, wincing as I imagined she did with each step. Together, her footprints and I walked beyond the small chain-link fence, around the Dumpster, and toward the street.

Tears pooled in my eyes. I envisioned pregnant Julieta placing her tender feet over the same stones that crunched under my shoes in the street. She walked to the restaurant on the other side of the road. I am color-blind, but sadly, I could follow every bloody step she took. I kicked a stone and watched it roll haplessly across the pavement.

I wandered back into the office and found a different set of red footprints, Ivanna's. Hers were in the hallway. The police told me Davis shot her when she made her way to the alarm panel. She managed to exit the building, bleeding from a gunshot wound and severe burns.

Placing my hands on my knees, I began to cough. Smoke and ash filled my lungs. I sucked in air, grieving for what was. I bent my knees and hugged myself; if I weren't so distraught, I would have been proud. It was a cold irony; Ivanna had done what I taught her to do in a panic situation. She entered the duress code at 3:39. Her red blood tinted the buttons, a lump of torn flesh stuck to the number 9. Bullet holes lined the same wall. I didn't know that so much blood could be left behind. I shivered with the thought of her fear.

Heartbroken and heavy, I returned to the Lakeland office. The CEO of Nationwide phoned. I refused to take his call. The Florida State Insurance Commissioner rang. I didn't talk to him either. I was simply too angry, too numb.

The office was a hive of activity. A team of agents (some mine, some from nearby agencies, and a few state-level Nationwide representatives) were already writing workers' compensation claims for their associates, ordering trucks to remove the burnt files and bloody furniture and accomplishing other tasks necessary during a catastrophe—finding a roofing company, a window replacement crew, and fire and water restoration teams who could help prevent further building damage.

There was a guy named George Laney, Nationwide's second-in-command in the state of Florida, who came to help.

"Scott," George said as he tipped his head and placed his hand on my shoulder. It should have comforted me. I should have been thankful for the guidance of a sympathetic voice. "Scott, staff, let's gather together. We are a team, a family," he said. George's demeanor was gentle and patient; his strength, evident. He held out his arms and motioned for the group to do the same.

Slowly, everyone joined hands. I stayed where I sat, alone on a bench in the corner, blinded by grief.

"Scott," George asked, "would you like to say a few words?"

I looked at a roomful of people, hand in hand, looking back at me. My rheumy eyes impossible to disguise, I spoke through broken sobs. "I don't have any answers." My chest heaved as I licked away salty tears. "I don't have a plan. I don't know what to do." I was defeated.

George asked if I wanted to pray. I answered bluntly, "No, no, I don't."

I've always been an on-again, off-again churchgoer. But I've never been on and off with my religion or my god. I spent time in prayer, meditating over scriptures, communicating with God. Sometimes, I would be involved with the physical church; other times I wouldn't. Each time I'd return, I felt as though I never left. At that moment, on Friday, December 14, I asked myself if I could pray when God had clearly left us powerless.

God had provided me with strength and direction my entire life. I would often tell people we were a Christian organization. Our company principles were guided by the teachings of Christ—follow the golden rule; do not cheat, steal, or kill; and pray without ceasing. I sat alone, with my hands on my knees, and cried. I heard George lead the prayer and simultaneously felt discarded and rejected.

On Monday, four days after the fire, I poked around the Lakeland office, wearied and spent. I saw a stack of newspapers dating back to Friday. The fire made the front page. There were pictures and articles filled with some information I knew and some I didn't. A photo of Ivanna's cousin and a former staff member, embraced and hysterical. A crystal clear photo of the Christmas tree through the broken window. Emergency personnel performing various responsibilities. Leon Davis.

"Scott, don't read it," one of my employees said.

I was sitting on the rocking chair in my private office across from the small kitchen. The wooden desk in the center was neat. My phone, silent on the corner, waited patiently as I fumbled with the newspaper. The lights were dim, and my eyes strained to read in the darkness and burned from four tearful, restless nights.

I had to read it. I had not looked at a newspaper or a television report. I had not done much but exist. One headline read, "Invader Burns 2 Women at Lake Wales Business; Police say robber threw gasoline onto employees, who are in critical condition."[2]

Taking a shallow breath, I read on. Julieta and Ivanna were flown to Orlando. Lake Wales police Captain Troy Schulze said it was "heartless, absolutely heartless." Leon Davis turned himself in. The article continued. I turned to another page only to see a photo of me in a dark-colored Headley Insurance shirt with my sunglasses perched on top of my head. My downturned mouth and heavy eyes showed my shock and fear. The caption read, "Insurance Agency Owner surveys his fire-damaged building in Lake Wales on Thursday after a robber set two women employees on fire, injuring them critically."[3]

Wrath shot through me. My grief turned to rage, my hands no longer trembling but now clutching the edges of the paper.

"Did you see this?" Shouting to nobody in particular, I threw the paper onto the desk. "This. Is. Not. Right."

A staff member, who had gone to the refrigerator for a bottle of water, came in and looked over my shoulder.

"This caption is not right." I could feel the heat rising in my cheeks. "This, this reporter," I stuttered. "This is not right." I huffed and opened another paper. The same photo stared back at me with a slightly different headline. "Here's another one! 'Headley Insurance Agency owner Scott Headley looks sullenly at his burned business as investigators wander the parking lot.'"[4]

"Scott, it's just a newspaper." She tried to sound soothing.

"Just a newspaper? Isn't a newspaper supposed to report the truth?" I emphasized the word truth. "Some people put a lot of trust in reporters."

"It's a caption."

"No. It's. Not. This is a front-page article. This is some reporter's opinion. People are going to read this and think an insurance agent only cares about his building. That's bullshit."

"Scott." She flinched at my word choice. Usually, I'm quick with laughter rather than profanity.

"You know what she was doing? She was prinking."

"What?"

"Prinking, printing and thinking. This is an insensitive comment. What about my employees? I couldn't give a damn about my building." My voice rose higher, more agitated, more pointed. The words came quick and sharp. "Ivanna and Julieta were life-flighted to a hospital, covered in burns, and this reporter says 'I'm assessing my building'?"

I could see my associate chew on the inside of her lip. We were all under stress, each of us handling the horror show differently. I yelled. She stood and listened.

"You know what I'm going to do? I'm going to not-so-politely ask this reporter to assess my fire-ridden building with me."

"Scott."

"You watch me."

I wrote down the reporter's name and found a phone number to the newspaper. I dialed.

She answered. I offered her an earful. "First of all, you don't know me, and your assumption of what you thought I was thinking was wrong."

"Mr. Headley—"

"I was standing there watching the first responders. I didn't even know that building existed," I interrupted before she could speak again. "That building could have been abducted by aliens for all I knew. I wasn't looking at the building. I was thinking about Ivanna and Julieta. The building's still there, and I want you to bring your opinionated ass out to meet me. I'm going to show you the incinerator my employees were burned in. I want you to see their fingernails stuck on the wall. You want my opinion of what I was thinking? You leave your camera at home and you leave your notebook at home and you meet me at two o'clock if you have any guts whatsoever."

I slammed the phone and drove to Lake Wales. She never showed. I sat and waited for an hour and a half. I was an angry person.

IVANNA AND JULIETA

The baby didn't make it. Born at just one pound two ounces via cesarean section, Michael Barrera made his debut into the world eighteen weeks premature. He was a fighter, living for three days without the affectionate touch of his mother. But that didn't mean he wasn't loved. Just before the fire, Julieta had proudly posted on her Myspace page she was waiting for her angel. The prophetic words haunted me, leaving me dull and achy.

The dull aches became magnified and complicated by a cough. In the immediate aftermath of the fire, the cold or flu I had been fighting, the one that prevented me from working on December 13, turned into an acute case of bronchitis. I visited the doctor with fever, chills, and breathing difficulties. I received treatment. My lungs began to heal. And I was heartbroken about it.

The seriousness of Ivanna's and Julieta's injuries compounded my broken heart. Their families set up camp at the hospital and discouraged anybody other than kin from visiting—including me. Finally, five days after the fire, I drove to the Orlando Medical Center and sat outside the intensive care unit. The sterile smell of rubbing alcohol and surface cleaner permeated the air. Nurses and doctors wandered about, talking in small whispers. I was on the mend while they lay comatose in the ICU.

"Scott, would you like to see Ivanna and Julieta?" Bruce Barrera asked as we shook hands. "We are all taking turns. They will only let us visit a few minutes at a time."

Bruce was Julieta's fiancé and father of Baby Michael. He was also Ivanna's brother. Ivanna and Julieta had grown up together in a small Texas community before moving to Florida separately. Julieta had two daughters from a previous relationship, but when she moved to Lake Wales, she and Bruce became an immediate family.

I looked at Bruce and thought of his broken heart. Both his sister and fiancée had been the victims of a horrific crime, and now, both were in the intensive care unit. I knew from the chitchat at work how close these two families were.

I always consider my employees family. Here, however, I sat alone, surrounded by people. I didn't know anyone, really. I had met Julieta's and Ivanna's fiancés and kids a few times. They were my girls, but I was out of place.

"It's okay, Scott," Bruce repeated at my hesitation. "You can go when it's my turn. I know how much Julieta and Ivanna loved you."

I wanted to see them; I needed to see them. I hoped that they could tell me what happened. I wanted to tell them I was on my way when Davis locked the doors. I wanted to tell them I was sorry I was late.

The truth is, I wasn't on my way to Lake Wales when Davis locked the door; I didn't have a crystal ball that could have prevented this god-awful tragedy. And I couldn't save them—then or now. But that knowledge did not absolve my conscience. The doctors had told us their time was limited. The burns covered over 90 percent of their bodies, each; victims don't recover from these types of burns.

I held Bruce's hand and looked into his eyes. If the situation were reversed, I would rather the time be spent with my loved ones than my boss. It was a reality I understood even though they seemed like family.

"No, Bruce," I responded. "But thank you." His offer was generous. Instead, I sat by myself, head down, hands clasped tightly on my knees, and I prayed to a god I was mad at.

* * *

Ivanna died five days after the fire. My heart numbed as I recalled how she proudly decorated her workstation with homemade art from her children. On the wall, she filled an entire bulletin board with photographs. She never missed an opportunity to take a picture or show one off. Ivanna had a way of making everything fun, whether it was playing bingo or cooking; she laughed through it all. Right then, I would have given anything to hear it again.

I lived in an altered universe. What should have been an exciting time, the days leading up to Christmas, were filled with struggle. Time would pass slowly, each tick of the clock's hand a reminder of my grief. Simple tasks, such as getting dressed or brushing my teeth, became monumental—requiring all my concentration and energy. I ate to live and drank to numb the pain. I thought I knew sorrow; I thought I understood it. But my sadness was more than melancholy; it was a chest-aching heaviness that blurred my vision and sapped my vitality.

On December 20, somebody arranged a prayer vigil. A pastor from a local church delivered a touching sermon, "Evil has darkened our day," he said, "and taken from us loved ones." At one point, we all sang a hymn and marched in a parade around the burned-out Headley building. The street teemed with people. Some I knew—my wife and children, my extended family and close friends, my office staff of past and present employees. In fact, more than four hundred people attended the service. Most people were strangers to me and created a sea that flooded the street and parking lot. They left stuffed animals and baby clothing and flowers and signs at the doorstep and on the sidewalk.

I tried to remain composed, hiding my emotions from everyone. I was unsuccessful and broke into sobs with everybody else. My most vivid memory is when my coworkers and family huddled close together, protective of me. We held one another up, or maybe, they just held me up.

I wish I could remember if the sky was blue and the birds sang. I wish I could have watched Ivanna play with her children, who were crying instead of laughing. Ivanna and her fiancé didn't have the chance to marry, and instead of celebrating life, we were mourning loss. With a strangled voice, I answered questions for a news crew. "This is family," I told them. "It's always been that way with us. This is people loving people. We share everything together. The building means nothing. My girls meant everything. That's the thing that hurts. I love them . . . We've got to start healing. We've got to stick together . . . I just appreciate everybody." Then a camera snapped a photo, another picture for posterity's sake.[5]

* * *

The newspaper reported that Ivanna died on December 18 at 10 p.m., just hours after I had visited the hospital.[6] A few days later, a simple obituary listed her family and the location of services. It also showed her to be a twenty-six-year-old manager of Nationwide Insurance. It left out her Cinderella story.

I had met her at a fast-food restaurant I frequented. She worked the lunchtime drive-through shift. Each time I'd see her, I'd tease her and say she didn't need a speaker. She would laugh and tease me back. She was boisterous and very unpolished. She also had a healthy set of lungs and a spark.

Each time I drove through, I gabbed with Ivanna. Over time, I looked forward to her greetings.

"Scott," my office manager said as I recalled my various meetings of Ivanna, "she's my cousin."

"What? How did I not know this?"

I insisted on an interview. Ivanna was even more vibrant outside the drive-through window, and I hired her. Once she came on board, talking in an office environment was the hardest thing to train Ivanna to do.

Her early assignments included simple filing and organization, skills she mastered quickly. Ivanna developed a rapport with our clientele. She spent quality time with each customer. She could explain policies and benefits thoroughly. She passed her licensing exam easily and, eventually, replaced her cousin as the Lake Wales office manager.

Often customers would come to discuss their policies and then linger just to have a conversation with Ivanna about children, motherhood, and family. They loved her; they looked forward to visiting with her. They laughed with her.

Ivanna's laugh wasn't a giggle or snicker, it was a hearty chuckle. Each time I heard it, I laughed. She didn't hide her Latina heritage. Long brown wavy hair surrounded her round face and deep, dark eyes. She would throw her head back and shake, so I would only see her chin. And she would chuckle louder. I'd laugh and say, "God forbid anybody says anything funny in the car, Ivanna, 'cause you're wreckin'!" She'd laugh and throw her head back again. I repeated that notion so often that it became our not-so-inside joke.

Another wonderful quality of Ivanna's was her love for her boys. They were the light of her life. She'd babble and gush about her children every chance she had. She, Julieta, and the kids would watch telenovelas together and eat dinner—they had fun. It was special. As the office manager, Ivanna would take the company credit card and buy snacks. They weren't exactly snacks. Ivanna would make a Mexican fiesta complete with homemade salsa, refried beans, and fresh tortillas. I often teased her and said I wouldn't pay for meals, but I wouldn't have wanted it any other way.

In 2004, Hurricane Charley came to town. As a gadget geek, I had every emergency covered: gallons of water, flashlights and batteries, and two-way radios. I even bought an ice generator. At first, the category 3 storm was heading for Orlando, then Tampa, and the thing kept jumping around. We staffed adjusters, prepared for the storm, and watched various weather predictions. At one point, experts believed the eye of Charley would pass over Lakeland. Later, it finally made landfall in Punta Gorda, just south of Tampa. As the north side of the storm passed my home, the wind circling my house howled like a ghost lived in the chimney. Through the crack in a boarded-up window, I could see my neighbor's roof lifting to the sky.

For a split second, I was relieved Charley would not directly impact my home. But I knew it could decimate Lake Wales. And it did. High winds, heavy rain, and a passing tornado uprooted trees and power lines, smashed cars, and crushed homes.

Before the last of the hurricane winds blew, Ben Mitchell and I hit the road with all the supplies Ivanna would ever need. We even included a roof tarp and toys for her boys. The main road had been shut down. The police stopped us and notified us we couldn't pass. We showed them our insurance cards and explained we would travel the old highway.

They told us we were crazy, but we went anyway. We drove that minivan through flooded cow pastures and around fallen trees. We pulled in front of Ivanna's one-story, tin-roofed home. The muddy yard was littered with branches and toys. She spied our car and ran to embrace us. Her eyes grew to the size of silver dollars, excited to see us but amazed we came. I asked her how she could believe we wouldn't.

I reflected on that day and smiled. Ivanna had chuckled and gave me a hug and told me how much she appreciated all I'd done for her. When I hired her, she had four years' experience as a worker in a fast-food joint. She had only ever received a ten-cent raise. She went from a drive-through cashier to a licensed insurance agent and office manager. That was the story the obituary missed.

*   *   *

Sitting in the back of the funeral home, I watched person after person reach Ivanna's coffin—touch it, speak to it, kneel by it. There were nice words said, heartfelt elegies—but I don't remember them. I remember her mother and thought about the incredible burden she bore to bury a child. I couldn't help but stare. She released a piercing cry that filled the chapel from ceiling to floor. She moaned and covered her face with her hands, her body trembling until somebody took hold of her arm to lift her from the seat. Others rose and followed closely behind, speaking in low murmurs so the remaining congregants were unable to hear. I put myself in her shoes and knew there were no such words that could make the pain go away.

My walk to the casket is etched in my mind. I experienced a palpable anxiety: heart racing, head sweating, hands shaking. I approached the casket, afraid to look, afraid if I looked, Ivanna's death would be real. There would be no more laughing, no more hugs. If I looked, I would see her spark was gone.

Ironically, I remember my fear but cannot recall the details of Ivanna's viewing. I think she wore a black dress and was covered in a veil. I believe her nephew, Julieta's son—three-day-old Baby Michael—lay next to her. I'm frustrated that these details are gone, but the memory does funny things during a traumatic event. She might have had a closed casket; Baby Michael might have been buried elsewhere. I can't recall.

After the service, my team huddled together, shook hands with Ivanna's family and friends, and consoled one another. But the media sensation of the story—the deliberate burning of Ivanna and Julieta, Baby Michael's short and tragic life—made for great headlines. Joining us were four Nationwide officers. They were there to field reporters' questions, to act as a physical barrier between the media and the funeral attendees, to direct camera flashes and microphones away from Ivanna's and Julieta's families and friends. But this meant keeping me away from the Barreras as well.

I've been told that funerals offer closure, a catalyst for healing. Once the funeral ended, a processional moved to the graveyard. I didn't go. I felt self-conscious and out of place. I didn't feel welcomed or part of anything. I only felt a deep, abiding emptiness.

I drove to the fast-food joint where I first met Ivanna. Outside on a bench nearby sat an older woman, hair matted and clothes tattered and unkempt. Instead of using the drive-through, I parked. "You look hungry," I said as I exited the truck.

"No, sir, I'm fine." She had an emaciated frame, but behind her dirty skin, her eyes were bright and patient.

"How about a cheeseburger? I'm going inside. Do you want to come in with me?"

"No, no, no. I'm comfortable out here."

"Okay. If I bought you a burger, would you eat it?"

She smiled and shook her head. I bought her one anyway, and a few minutes later, she had a jumbo-size meal in her hands.

"God bless you, sir," she said as she took the bag and pulled it toward her chest.

I nodded and unlocked my truck. I didn't feel blessed.

* * *

Julieta died on January 3, exactly three weeks after the birth of her baby. Immediately after the fire, she cried in pain and prayed for her baby's life. She had suffered third- and fourth-degree burns over 90 percent of her body. Before the robbery, I knew nothing of fourth-degree burns.

While they inflict the most damage, after the sensation of the first- and second-degree burns, third and fourth are painless because the nerves and surrounding tissue have already died. When the paramedics placed Julieta on the gurney, I later found out, she was calm. They administered medicine to help ease her suffering and prevent the risk of infection; she fell into a coma. Michael was born, but she never woke up. Her best friend died, but she never woke up.

Julieta was buried in Texas after a ceremony held in Lake Wales. I know I attended the ceremony because there is a photo of me in the paper, but I don't remember it. Time began to blur. Sleepless nights and agonizing days, I was haunted by the senseless act of burning someone alive. Someone who had been so shy I almost didn't hire her.

Julieta did not fit my typical new-hire profile. I search for people who exude confidence and energy—people like Ivanna. I had met Julieta a few times. She was quiet and timid. "Scott, trust me!" Ivanna laughed at my hesitation. "I know Julieta. You'll be impressed." She smiled and laughed again. She had persistence and disarmed my reluctance. Ivanna was the new Lake Wales office manager, and I knew for her to succeed, I should trust her intuition. In 2005, Ivanna hired Julieta, and Ivanna was right. Julieta was honest and hardworking and a great addition to the agency. Our team is a friendly group; we would cheer one another on and offer pats on the back. Around me, Julieta remained shy and uncertain of herself—speaking softly, avoiding eye contact, smiling instead of saying hello.

In contrast to Ivanna's daily hugs, Julieta would softly say, "Hi, Scott," or, "Bye, Scott." But the clients loved her. She laughed easily with them, listened to their stories, and shared some of her own. She learned office procedures quickly and had just qualified to take the Florida State Insurance License Exam, which can often take several hours of schooling. I was able to mentor her, instead, as an insurance agency owner. I was confident in her knowledge and even more impressed with the way she made each client feel valued. Clients often told me Julieta offered them sage advice; they trusted her and asked for her counsel. That is a quality that training can't teach.

On December 12, I visited the Lake Wales office. As I left, Ivanna, as always, gave me a hug and told me she was glad to see me. I gave Julieta a side hug and patted her belly.

"Julieta, I think something's come between us," I joked.

Julieta shook her head and smiled. "Scott, I think it's always been there." She laughed and rubbed my own small paunch.

I had big plans for Julieta. I was proud of her accomplishments and intended to give her a large raise once she passed her test. But that day didn't come.

WILL EARNHARDT

About two weeks after the fire, I received a phone call from a Nationwide litigations claims manager. It would be this person's position to manage any civil legal claims that might be on the horizon because of complex personal and property-damage claims. A litigations claims manager would offer me guidance, help respond to legal questions from lawsuits, and coordinate with any defense counsel if necessary.

At that time, I was not taking phone calls. I didn't speak to the Florida State Insurance commissioner. I didn't speak to the president of Nationwide Insurance. I sat in my office, with the lights out. But God works in mysterious ways.

"Hey, Scott, I'm Will Earnhardt. I wanted to tell you how sorry I am and I'm praying for you and your whole team."

"Thanks." I had picked up the phone. I listened. I nodded in silent thought.

"I want you to know I've been assigned as a litigations claims manager by Nationwide for any civil storm that comes your way."

"That won't happen."

"It might. In sensational cases like this. Litigation nation."

"You mean like O. J. Simpson. They didn't convict him of his ex-wife's murder but found him guilty in a civil trial."

"Something like that. Civil suits happen for a lot of different reasons. But they are on a timeline. Statute of limitations. And sometimes they have nothing to do with the criminal trial."

"There's no reason why anyone would sue Headley for this. How could they?"

"Well, if some lawyer comes knocking, just let me know. Keep my information in your back pocket. Call me if you need anything."

"Sure, thanks for the call."

I breathed out a slight laugh. As if anybody would sue us.

Dead to the World

Before the robbery, bedtime was one thing I enjoyed more than anything else in the world. Soft cotton pajamas covered in superhero logos, fresh linens, and pillows piled a mile high. I'd snuggle into the sheets with my wife, and she would gently scratch my back, then I'd gently scratch hers. We'd been married over twenty years, and I knew her quirks like the back of my hand. As she would quietly fall asleep, I'd twirl her hair and watch as her body would slowly sink into slumber. She'd jerk and twitch for a few seconds, and she'd be out before the lights. Our days were busy, but our quality time was comfort time.

Some nights, I'd open a thick spy-thriller paperback, broken at the spine with dog-eared pages. I'd relax, read a little, then set down my book and open my Bible. I'd review a scripture and talk to God until my eyelids fell heavy. Dimming the lights, I would drift to slumber. It wasn't about going to sleep; it was about my downtime with my wife, with God, with my own thoughts. My ritual was so perfected it was as if I were a trained professional.

After the robbery, sleep seemed more a myth than a possibility. My mind would race with thoughts of doubt, of my ineffectiveness to move through my own pain. Unlike the image of Superman on my pj's, I couldn't go rewind time to change the future. The first week, I slept maybe a total of ten hours. If I were awake, I was crying. I'd reluctantly lie in bed, twisting and turning, tears streaming down my cheeks. My grief was bubbling at the surface.

On March 26, 2007, my mom died. I don't know *why* she died. As the most stubborn of her three children, I refused to allow an autopsy and forced my siblings to sign paperwork agreeing to that. I already knew *how* she died; she quit breathing. The rest was immaterial. Her death was quick and untimely. It left a hole in my heart I ignored with my nose to the grindstone.

On September 24, 2007, my grandmother died. She'd lived a good life—long and prosperous. Although no death is easy, my grandmother died from congestive heart failure at the age of eighty-six—her death was easier to process than my mother's. My two maternal guiding lights gone just before I needed them the most; I had barely started to grieve when Leon Davis flicked his lighter.

Now, after the robbery and fire, the hole I tried to fill with long hours of toil was ripped wide open. Grief consumed me; sleep abandoned me. I felt crazy and knew I would go insane. I considered pills but opted for booze. I'd drink a beer or two—or eighteen—trying to dull my senses. Eventually, I would pass out drunk, not bothering to set an alarm clock. My arms and legs felt entrapped in cement while my head would cycle through the same events repeatedly. Sometimes I wouldn't go to the office until noon or one. I didn't have any desire to be at work. I didn't have any desire to work. I didn't have any desire to be associated with anything.

Maybe, if I passed out, if my brain were foggy enough, I would sleep through the nightmares. The nightmares were intense and always different: they never took place in Lake Wales or included Ivanna or Julieta. I never once saw Leon Davis. But they were always in battle; I was always pinned down—fight or flight. I was always trying to protect somebody.

They were the most vivid dreams I had ever had. One night I dreamed I was dead. I couldn't leave this earth until I could get somebody to bury me. I could feel the moist clumps of dirt wedged between my fingers. I could smell the iron-laden mud stuck between my toes.

Nobody would cover me with soil. In my dream, everybody thought I had lost my mind. I didn't appear dead. But I was as dead as dead got. I wanted out; I wanted to move on, but nobody would bury me. The more I tried to persuade them, the angrier I became. I woke up visibly upset, sweaty, my hands and feet sore, my legs twisted in damp sheets. I stumbled to the bathroom and washed my face. The mirror reflected someone I didn't recognize, a man with hollow eyes and pallid skin. I wandered to the kitchen and poured a glass of milk. I sipped it slowly, fearing my return to bed, knowing the dream would pick up right where it left off.

LEON DAVIS JR.

The old RV appeared in the Lake Wales parking lot one week after the robbery. It belonged to Dave Dershimer, another Nationwide Insurance agent who lived in the area. A dank, musty smell permeated every inch of the twenty-foot beast. Like most motor homes, it had a bed and built-in captain's chairs and a kitchen table. A faded velour couch sat across the main door where the work crew would conduct business. It became my refuge, a place I could avoid everyone with a simple twist of a lock. And I was grateful for it.

The Lake Wales office had been closed, but things were still happening on the property. Rudimentary cleanup and repair required little supervision, and someone taped a note to the replacement window. Handwritten on a large piece of brown cardboard was a notice: "Due to circumstances beyond our control . . ." But nothing seemed in my control. I gathered up newspapers from the previous week and took them along with a six-pack of beer to the trailer. I opened a beer and began to read. The *Ledger*, Polk County's local newspaper, ran dozens of articles about Leon Davis Jr. and Ivanna and Julieta. Davis had a history of criminal offenses. Through the anger and tears, I read the articles, trying to understand how someone could be so cruel.

Apparently, immediately after the fire began, a countywide search for Leon Davis using the media, helicopters, and the Lake Wales Police and PSCO—Polk County Sheriff's Office—began. Davis turned himself in four hours after the start of the fire, on the eve of his thirtieth birthday. According to one article, he told someone at the sheriff's office, "I hurt somebody, I swear I hurt somebody."[7] By all accounts, he didn't seem like a vicious criminal—before.

To his friends and family, Davis was a fun guy. He was reliable and kind. He had a child with Down syndrome and had a baby on the way. People thought of him as a good dad, someone who was living the American Dream.

Ha! The man who committed such heinous acts was none of those things. I didn't care that he lived in suburbia. He was a monster, and I wanted justice for Ivanna and Julieta. He turned his dream into my nightmare.

Regardless of the kind things people said, he had a past. In 2002, he and his then-girlfriend were caught stealing Easter eggs from Walmart. Davis, the father of a boy who was two at that time, probably wanted a nice celebration for his child. As time progressed, he began to wear flashy jewelry. He bought a house. There's even a newspaper photo of a grinning Davis with large diamond studs in his ears. He leveraged himself, it seemed, beyond his financial means.

In December 2006, he and his fiancée began robbing Sam's Club by purchasing items, keeping the original, but returning with the receipt and collecting the same item at the door and returning the unpurchased one. It was a scheme that netted them over $2,400 before capture in January 2007.

At one point, he quit his job at Florida's Natural, an orange juicing plant in Lake Wales, and took a less-paying job as part of a maintenance team for the city of Eagle Lake, another nearby community. A short time later, a mere eleven months after being arrested for stealing from Sam's Club, he was arrested for stealing over $11,000 worth of orange juice from Florida's Natural. While it seems improbable, even impossible, several pallets went missing. Davis apparently purchased four pallets personally but delivered a total of fifteen to his cousin's restaurant in Lake Wales[8]. He was charged with grand theft, thrown in jail, and subsequently suspended from his job in Eagle Lake, leaving him broke.

Just three days after his release from jail on December 3, 2007, two men working at a Lake Alfred BP station were murdered, each shot at close range in the head, while changing the outside marquee. The coroner called them execution-style murders: Davis had complete control; the victims had no way to escape. It was ruthless, and at that time, the PCSO suspected the murderer would both rob and kill again.

Before the Headley robbery and desperate for information, the PCSO announced a $12,000 reward for information about the murders. The sheriff even made a video appeal to Polk County's inmate population:

> This is Sheriff Grady Judd. Would you all like to have a very merry Christmas? Well, I can't let you all out of jail, but I can do this: I can make sure you have $12,000 cash. You can remain totally anonymous. And all I need is a piece of information. I need to know who executed

two people December the 7th at approximately 9:00 p.m. at an attempted store robbery. I know you've been locked up, but what about your friends and family? I can promise you this: no follow-up, no testifying in court. Just call Crime Stoppers or have your family call. I'll guarantee you $12,000 cash just to point us in the right direction. We need your help. Thanks.[9]

While the transcript of the plea is somewhat jovial, it was a fearful testimony to know somebody like this might live in our community, a community where everybody knows everyone else. It was even worse to know that this man was now linked to the robbery and fire—and a previous Headley customer.

By the time I read about Davis, he had already been connected to these murders, and his weeklong crime binge had been dubbed the worst killing spree in Polk County history. The Sheriff's office even reported that Davis talked to "people at a local business about the shooting. He [told] them that if the Patels had handed over the money, they wouldn't have been shot."[10] My anger and frustration mounted. I recalled the comment Chief Gillis made about the similarities between the "Lake Alfred case" and the robbery. At the time Gillis made his comment, I thought he was a genius, a soothsayer, a psychic. He was none of those things, but he was an intuitive police officer. The law enforcement community feared the killer would strike again. He did, at my place of business.

Frightened by reality, I lay down on the old mattress. I had become cranky and detached. I wanted the whole scenario to vanish, to return to normal. *I* wanted to return to normal. I wanted to tell stupid knock-knock jokes and watch people laugh. I wanted to pick up my rifle and go skeet shooting. I wanted to shoot pool with my buddies. Instead, I prayed. *Prayed* was not the right word—praying implies I had a two-way conversation with God. I did not. I was talking *at* God; I was not listening. That's not correct either. I was not on speaking terms with him. I guess I was talking to a teddy bear somebody brought into the trailer.

I curled into a ball, cradled the bear, and talked. I fell into a familiar trance. The shock, the fear, the death of people so young. People who lived an ordinary life by waking up each morning and kissing their loved-ones good-bye as they left for work. People who expected to go home at the end of the day and wake up the next morning to do it all over again. Instead, they were terrorized, engulfed in flames, shot, and helpless to stop it. I was helpless to stop it.

A car drove past. It slowed, and I peeked out the cloth venetian blinds. I watched a police cruiser pass. Since the robbery, the Lake Wales police department retained a constant vigil over our building. They parked their cruisers in the back parking lot overnight and kept vandals and looters away. It helped me feel protected—on the surface. I laid my head back onto the cushion.

A few moments later, another car slowed. A woman parked in the street, exited her car, and laid a pile of baby clothes on the sidewalk. She knelt and crossed herself before she returned to her automobile. Her offering was not the first to be left at the curb, and she was not the first to wipe the snot off her nose. People had been driving to the burned-out building, stopping, and leaving gifts since the day after the robbery.

Signs, "We miss you, Ivanna and Julieta," "Our prayers are with you," hand drawn and simple, slowly appeared, then clothes and toys, flowers, stuffed animals, and tears. We were covered in a shroud of grief that began to engulf everyone around for miles. With each sign I read, I relived my drive from home to Lake Wales on December 13. What-if's scattered through my mind. What if I had been there? What could I have done? I pushed my nose into the teddy bear and tried to smell Ivanna's homemade flautas instead of the stale motor home mattress.

I attempted to avoid the media. Stories of Ivanna, Julieta, and Leon Davis dominated the newspapers; they played daily on the nightly news. Like a car accident—I didn't want to rubberneck, but I couldn't look away. To me, it was 9/11 all over again. If the television was on, I watched it. If a newspaper article appeared, I read it. If someone came to visit, we'd talk about it. It was unbearable to watch and difficult to escape. Lake Wales was not *the City that Never Sleeps*, but it, too, was a community that had been shaken by a devastating tragedy.

I lay huddled with the teddy bear, haunted by media images. My employees, lighthearted Ivanna and sweet Julieta, floated through my mind. I wanted to remain hidden from the world, locked in the trailer, hugging a teddy bear. But tomorrow the sun would rise and life would continue. Peeking at the building in ruins, I needed to make decisions about the business. The most obvious one: keep the office open or closed.

I had the option of closing the Lake Wales office forever, moving locations, or staying on West Central Avenue. To shutter is to quit, to give up—the easy way out—the coward's way out. I could move to another location. That was appealing, a fresh start, without the ghastly memories of yellow tape and fire trucks or the rusty, metallic smell of blood.

My third choice was to remain, to rebuild, to make it more secure, more robust. I opened the camper door, holding the bear under my arm, and watched an ibis with his curved beak and white feathers hunt for worms. This was his home. The events of December 13 didn't scare him away.

RESTORATION

"Ben!" I barked into the phone. Ben Mitchell, my friend, former coworker, and relative helped secure the building in the immediate aftermath of the fire. I asked him to rejoin the agency, to lend a hand in rebuilding the Lake Wales office, to bring it back to life. I was grateful he said yes.

"Ben, we've got to meet."

I paced, both nervous and excited, over the asphalt parking lot. I stopped at the low hedgerow between the pavement and the sidewalk and absentmindedly brushed my hand over the top of the bushes. I had made a decision.

"I want a sign," I said when he finally arrived.

"A sign?"

"Yes, I want it to say Resolve, Courage, Hope."

"Resolve, Courage, Hope?" he asked.

We walked toward the front of the burned-out building.

"I want it right here." I raised my hands and gestured to the sky. "A big sign for everybody to see."

Ben looked at me and smiled. He might have thought I was crazy.

"Resolve," I continued, "we're going to do this. We're going to rebuild."

Ben nodded.

"Courage, I have no clue where we're going to get that." I knew bravery is something that is a result of stepping outside of fear. Bravery needed courage, and I was sure courage would be difficult to find. Again, Ben nodded. "And hope? I don't even know if it exists." My voice rose higher, uncovering my own dread of such a daunting project. It seemed like years since the office had been vibrant. I looked at the piles of offerings left to Ivanna, Julieta, and Baby Michael. The decision to rebuild was frightening and hung over me like a wet baby blanket sitting on the curb. There is no courage without fear, hope for a better tomorrow, and the resolve to see it through. While I needed all three, courage seemed the most important.

I turned to face the building, a duplex with a stone front facade. My dad's building. When I bought his business, he remained owner of the duplex. The left side housed Headley Insurance. We had plans to expand, to use the whole building. Mercifully, when the fire was set, the right side had been vacant.

A Christmas wreath hung in between two identical brown wooden doors. The hole in the blue-asphalt roof and the broken windowpanes were already repaired. Except for the new brown roof, the outside of the building looked the same as it had before the fire. I swung around and faced the street. Past the small hedgerow of bushes, the baby clothes the woman left sat next to a large pile of stuffed animals, real and silk flowers, balloons, and candles. They all lay scattered from one end of the sidewalk to the other. Nailed to a curbside palm tree hung the signs declaring love and well-wishes.

"Come with me," I commanded. Ben turned and trailed me. We stepped toward the makeshift shrine. I grabbed a handful of items and headed to a bin behind the office. "We need to get rid of these."

Ben scampered alongside me, grabbing handfuls of teddy bears and flowers.

"It's not going to be depressing like this," I said, breathing deeply. I rushed to the Dumpster, filled with adrenalin. "I'm not going to let the Headley Building become a monument to sadness. We are not giving in to fear. This is not going to remain our ground zero."

* * *

Bill Bair called a month after the fire. I had begun to avoid the media, but Bill had a special place in my heart. During the fire, I became visibly ill. I crawled on all fours and vomited. Bill was the man who shielded me from the crowd, the one who hid me from the snapping cameras. I was left with a feeling of shame. I hadn't been helpful or strong enough for Ivanna and Julieta, vomiting instead of rescuing. I might have had the flu and a nasty bout of bronchitis, but that knowledge did little for my pride.

No one knows how they will respond during a traumatic event. While I was kneeling on all fours in a paved parking lot, Bill had been my guardian angel. His presence helped me hold on to a small amount of dignity. When he asked for an interview, I said yes. In reality, I hated the media. They followed me around like flies to a trash truck. My first encounter was during the fire—cameras clicking, noses sticking where they didn't belong. My photo had been in so many papers across the country I became a household image: The man whose associates burned to death. Look, there he is, assessing his building.

I had been interviewed at the fire, at funerals, and at the prayer vigil. I was at a disadvantage. People thought they knew me—Scott Headley of the Headley Insurance Fire. My persona and my business seemed to be synonymous to everybody I would see on the street. Or maybe I was morphing into a man I barely recognized, stoic and strong on the outside, mourning and distressed on the inside.

But I was just a man with a business. In 1999, with a young family, I moved from West Virginia to Florida to work for my father, who, at that time, owned Headley Insurance Corporation.

In my eyes, my dad was larger than life. I always looked at him as the sturdiest rock in the world. He was tough and aggressive. A go get 'em, cutthroat type of man, somebody you didn't want to mess with but somebody you wanted to learn from. Instead of giving me a nickel, he gave me an opportunity. And I welcomed it. It had been his dream for us to work together: father and son, taking on the world. After years of persuasion, my wife and I finally agreed to move to Florida.

In 2006, my dad had a heart attack. I was already the managing partner of Headley Insurance Corporation and knew it was time to purchase the business from my father. In early 2007, I became the sole proprietor of Headley Insurance Agency LLC. My dad left the company and never looked back. He traveled, relaxed, and played round after round of golf. When Leon Davis walked into the office with a gas tank and a roll of duct tape, my dad was in Atlanta, enjoying his retirement.

One month after that, Bill Bair arranged a simple interview. When Bill arrived, he brought a videographer, and the three of us sat in the tired old motor home. I didn't realize the interview would be taped, but fortunately, I had worn my signature Headley Insurance oxford shirt and khakis.

Before taping began, Bill and I developed a nice rapport. I respected him as a journalist. He covered much of the ordeal—reporting on everything from the gruesomeness of the crime to the delicate news of Baby Michael's death. He was known as a journalist with integrity, and the gentle way he handled the tragedy was to be admired.

The video tech pulled the faded mauve curtains closed and hooked me up with a microphone. Bill sat opposite me. Somehow, the weathered RV— with its threadbare couches and musty carpeting—seemed an appropriate backdrop for this scruff of a man. His beard and bushy eyebrows accentuated his fatherly demeanor. He was unthreatening, even disarming with his soft Florida twang.

"You know," I started as I turned to face a teddy bear propped up on the washed-out refrigerator, "people still leave stuffed animals on the sidewalk and drop off children's clothes. It just shows me how much the community cares."

Bill nodded. "I see the sign, 'Resolve, Courage, Hope,' in the front of the building. Tell me about that sign."

"Bill, I'm just so blessed. We had the sign made to show the community we're coming back. I just wanted to thank everyone for their support. It's been humbling, really. It's obvious how much the girls were loved by everyone. The community's pulled together, offered support. When I speak with people, they want us back in Lake Wales, they want the office reopened."

Bill scribbled a note on a piece of lined paper. He looked up at me and smiled. "That's not just the people that knew them. That's everybody," he said.

"That's the spirit of the community. It's obvious we've felt the same emotion—it's just been an emotional roller coaster—but every time I seem to get really down, that phone call comes in, or a card, or an e-mail. Or someone just showing up and giving us a hug, and it's just really amazing."

I paused for what seemed an eternity. My eyes glanced around the room while I tried to swallow my grief. I tried to look resilient, for Bill, for my associates, for the community. "The families are amazing. We are a Christian organization. We are blessed with so many people in our organization who are saved and know God. That's really the only thing that can put you at ease in a time like this. Because of their faith and their love for the Lord, they went from pain to perfect in a breath, and it's a comforting feeling."

Again, I paused. I thought about my feelings for God—God, whom I was still mad at.

"Were the girls fun loving?" Bill asked.

"They were just wonderful ladies, so full of life, loved to laugh, just great mothers. They lived for their children. Ivanna had a contagious laugh. She'd start laughing, and you'd laugh with her and figure out what you were laughing at later on. She'd been here for six years."

"And Julieta?"

"Julieta was a great mother too. She was our newest employee. She'd been working here for two years."

"How many employees do you have altogether?"

"Twenty-one, in three offices. We're all like family. Even my wife and three children work here. The Lake Wales office has been here for twelve years."

"What about this camper?"

"It's just the greatest thing. Dave Dershimer, he operates an insurance agency in Winter Haven, donated it. You know, Bill, people have offered us office space elsewhere. But I want to be here for the customers." I swung my hand around to indicate this location. That Headley Insurance would be here, on this spot, just as it had been.

"This location seems to be special," Bill added.

"Clients come in every day. They want to talk about the mayhem. They come in crying and upset or angry at the situation. So many emotions, every day. We want to comfort them and offer hope." I held my breath for a second and rubbed my hand over my khakis. It seemed easy to comfort others, yet I felt inconsolable.

"How much damage did the building sustain?"

"About $100,000."

"You are going to open in the same location?"

"Not the exact same location. The offices will move to the east end of the building. It would be too painful to stay in the same suite. Moving next door seems to be the best option."

"That's good."

"I spent a lot of time praying about it, just trying to figure out, where do we go from here? This feels like our 9/11." I wrung my hands together to visualize our tragedy, our town, pulling together to support one another. "The way the community's responded, it's just humbling." I turned my head so Bill wouldn't see my misty eyes. "And that's when I just thought *resolve*. We have to have courage and hope. It hurts me to see people drive by the front and pause and just kinda hang their head and see how sad they are from a distance. I'm determined to build it back, to reopen, just to show what kind of resolve the people of Lake Wales have. That's what the girls would want. It's what they would be doing right now if this happened to another office."

Bill nodded.

I continued, "People feel they want to do something to help. It's absolutely amazing I've received cards and e-mails from all over the country—people I'll never meet." I said, my voice gravely, "Everyone has come together. It's important for us to reopen. Here, in the same place."

Bill leaned toward me and said, "Scott, thanks. That was great."

I took the mike off my lapel and handed it to the videographer, who was busy coiling up wires. They packed up the sound and video equipment while I stood and tried to move out of their way. We shook hands just before they drove away. I crawled back into the camper feeling hollow. [11]

* * *

Resolve. It was written on the sign for everybody to see. I suppressed my anxiety of reopening the office. My angst was stowed, deep within, and I forced myself to move through my days. I became useful again, no longer hugging teddy bears and watching for people to drive solemnly past the office. I had a daily routine of sorts: visit the main office in Lakeland, sort through files salvaged from the fire we'd moved to our third office on the other side of Lakeland, and inspect the construction in Lake Wales.

Each day I filled my truck with files and equipment and transported them from place to place. The truck was a loaded Nissan Nismo. Bucket seats, chrome and black interior, leather-wrapped steering wheel. Designed for off-road adventures, it sported big tires, external fog lights, and a roll bar. It was, by far, the nicest-looking truck I'd ever owned, and I put it to work.

The truck was a beauty, and I took good care of it, following up on all maintenance issues, regular oil changes and tire rotations, and never letting the gas gauge fall below one quarter, until now.

I drove steadily from one location to another. The tank's needle fell into the red zone. A gas station sat thirty yards ahead of me. My heart raced; my palms grew sweaty. I clenched my teeth and continued to drive straight past it. Panic washed over me like a tidal wave. Such a simple task, yet it unnerved me. I pictured a BP station, its green and white sign and the two men Davis assassinated. I imagined Ivanna and Julieta, duct-taped and splashed with fuel. I parked my car and closed my eyes. I smelled imaginary smoke and retched.

* * *

The main office ran on autopilot—or rather by the incredible professionalism and support of the Headley staff. They took over many of my responsibilities on top of their own. I entered, wandered to my desk in the back, closed the door, and stared at nothing in particular. While nestling my head in my hands, Larry Herbert, our longtime mail carrier, quietly tapped on the door.

"Hey Scott," he gently said. "I wanted you to know I'm still praying for you and Ivanna and Julieta. I wanted to give you some encouragement."

Larry had stopped by every day to drop off mail. If I were in, he would pop his head around the corner and tell me he was praying for me. His consistency buoyed me. "Thanks, man." I matched his kind voice, trying to sound encouraged when, in fact, I was scared and desperate for my agony to subside. I knew he'd served in Vietnam. I'm sure he understood the need for continued compassion, and I bet he had a story or two to share. But he never did. He just stopped by and smiled, dropped off the mail and wished us well.

"All right, then, you take care." I gratefully accepted his offered hand.

*   *   *

In another part of town, the third Headley building became the unofficial storeroom for machinery, furniture, and files. This small office was located in an industrial part of town surrounded by machine shops, auto-repair facilities, and a quiet Hispanic population.

At that time, we did not have an electronic office; the majority of our documents were paper and ink. I sifted through hundreds of records. I'd open a box and would immediately be overcome with the sour smell of rotting pulp. It clung to the files. Bits of black dust tainted the inside of my nose and stained my fingertips.

Slowly, I peeled apart pages. One by one, each page told a story—a summary of an interview or a policy change, names of clients who moved or passed away. The work was slow. I was tired from restless nights, was emotionally spent, and had a constant headache, but I was productive.

One file would have notes written in ink, Julieta's handwriting. Another would have Ivanna's. Occasionally, I would see a file with notes from both women. The process was incessant. The most disturbing files would be ones with a significant date and time written on it, such as Ivanna's date of birth.

Once, I wanted to do something special for Ivanna's birthday, to let her know how valuable she was to the team, how much we appreciated her, and how proud I was of all she had achieved. I invited the Lake Wales team to help celebrate at an upscale restaurant. A gregarious woman with a simple background, Ivanna lived without the spoils of excess, but her warmth and love of life was infectious.

Lake Wales is an old Florida town initially settled by the Lake Wales Land Company with the intention of growing citrus and processing turpentine in 1911. Situated 239 feet above sea level, it is one of the highest cities in Florida. Surrounded by almost six hundred freshwater lakes, it became the quasi-essential place to be in the 1920s. Mansions built by America's elite spread across the Lake Wales Ridge—an old, eroded mountain chain that was "beach front" over 650,000 years ago. One such example is Bok Tower and its neighbor Pinewood Estate. In 1921, *Ladies' Home Journal* editor Edward W. Bok decided to create a garden and bird sanctuary in Lake Wales. He commissioned Frederick Law Olmsted Jr.—the architect of the White House Gardens—to build a landscape that would emphasize the tranquil, sweeping vistas. Olmsted designed a 205-foot pink marble singing tower complete with carillon bells and a reflecting pond.

Next to Bok Tower is the former home of Charles Austin Buck, a former vice president of Bethlehem Steel Company. Constructed in 1932, Buck built El Retiro, as it was known at that time, so his bedroom window would open to Bok Tower and its formidable gardens. At almost thirteen thousand square feet with servant's quarters and two attached apartments, its lavish Spanish design had custom doors and windows. Eventually, it was bought by the Bok Tower Gardens, and together, the neighboring structures are now a National Historic Landmark.

But hurricanes and late-winter freezes have been hard on Lake Wales, and today, Lake Wales is a community where there is either old money or no money. Just down the road from Mountain Lake Estates, the ritzy part of town, lies a mixture of one-, two-, and three-bedroom homes with no landscaping, chain-link fences, and a desperate need for painting.

Dotted around the area are a handful of fast-food and chain restaurants. Instead of visiting one of these for Ivanna's birthday, I took the staff to a golf club restaurant, the same club that offered Edward Bok and Charles Buck golf, tennis, and croquet; far-reaching views of the mountain lake; and a dress code. The tables, draped in white linen cloth with cleverly folded napkins, were not out of place for this exclusive restaurant. We were promptly greeted by our server with freshly printed menus.

"Your table is this way," the hostess said.

I pulled out Ivanna's chair and casually sat next to her.

This was Ivanna's first visit to an upscale restaurant. She read the menu.

"Ivanna, this is your birthday. I'm going to get the steak. It's delicious. You love steak. Why don't you get one too?"

The server made notes and proceeded around the table. Bread and butter, salads and sodas were brought out first. We munched and laughed about nothing in particular. When the steaks arrived, it was perfection. Ivanna savored every bite. She laughed and complimented each mouthful as if she'd never had a steak before, adding, "This is so much better than fast food."

After finishing our meals, the server came over and began clearing the table.

"I can do this," Ivanna jumped up and started to remove the plates.

"No, no," the server insisted.

"Really, I can put this away for you. You sit here." Ivanna pulled out her chair for the server.

It was sweet; it was innocent. It was Ivanna, a woman who'd thought her fast-food job was all she would achieve. Sitting alone on the floor, my fingers stained with soot, haunted with this memory, I tried, unsuccessfully, not to cry.

* * *

Sorting through the muck and the mush, cinders and slag was menial yet very important. Boxes had been stacked high, pushed against the walls. The goal was to protect sensitive information such as social security numbers, addresses, and phone numbers. Policy information could be recreated, but identity theft was unacceptable.

I would enter the building and close the door, inside, an uncomfortable rancid smell. It permeated my clothes, much like an old, forgotten rag left in the rain and covered by a plastic bag. Box after box, the dampness left a film, tacky to the touch. Reaching into one box, I pulled a stack of files and, like a surgeon, delicately peeled each paper from the pile. Some files had been so damaged that all the patience in the world couldn't save them. They would sit in a box together; every file in that container was pulp—an ashen stew.

And each file offered me ghost stories.

Hey, Julieta, one file would say as I peeled one sheet of paper from another.

Yes, Ivanna?

Did you see Samuel when he came in yesterday?

Oh, girl, he was looking fine.

Shush, girl, you're taken.

Yes, but that doesn't mean I can't look. You obviously did!

I'd pull another page apart. And the voices would start again.

You know the woman who just drove past? Well, she's only driving a fancy car because she's gotten herself a new man.

Oh no, she didn't?

Oh yes, she did!

And an image of Ivanna, tossing back her hair and shaking her head, would materialize then fade away. Sorting became the most imperative task of my life, and it wasn't working out for me. I would go home and scrub the filmy residue off my skin until it was raw, returning the next day and repeating the process. Frustrated and exhausted, I'd finally had enough; I stood up and carried an unsalvageable box to the Dumpster. I tossed the box into the trash bin and screamed as loud as I could. "Ah, hell with this!" echoed off the walls and through the neighborhood.

I wanted to give up. My life, it seemed, was in the muck and the mush, and no matter how hard I tried to peel back the layers, I was left in tatters. People would tell me, "Time heals all wounds," or "God wouldn't give you anything you couldn't handle." At that moment, I couldn't handle the simple task of reclaiming paperwork. I wasn't sure if it were possible to reclaim my life.

CRISIS RECOVERY

I viewed the rebuild as a war zone recovery project with me as the general. Life was stark, and planning to attack the reconstruction was the escape from reality I needed. The Lake Wales office would not be ground zero, but rather the road to justice. It would be rebuilt, better, stronger, safer. Whatever I wanted, I got. As the construction ramped up, I became a person I've never been before: demanding, exacting, ornery.

The duplex, now vacant on both sides, was already fortified on the exterior. I stepped into the burned-out shell of the office. The walls still covered in blood and bullet holes, I tiptoed my way over melted carpeting and around crumbled drywall. It stank of decay.

"We are moving to the other side," I stated. I had made that decision the day I decided to rebuild. It was not an easy call. I had plans to knock down the wall and double the size of the office. Now, I wasn't sure; regardless of what I told Bill Bair in our interview, I wasn't sure anybody really wanted us back. But I pressed on. "But we are keeping our address."

The contractor nodded as we walked around the premises.

"And the bushes out front. Those are coming down." To me, dammit, they were the reason no one saw Leon Davis enter the building carrying a gas can.

He scribbled in his notebook as we proceeded through the building.

"And fix these holes," I said a bit too loudly and pounded my finger on the wall. "I don't need to be reminded Ivanna was *shot* in here."

Everything inside had to be replaced. When the contractor went to pull the permits, he applied using the 124 West Central Avenue address for the suite next door.

"Scott," he later said to me, "we aren't allowed to move sides."

"What the hell does that mean?" my temperament already on edge, I barked at the contractor.

"The city said you can't move because they have two different addresses."

"It's my damn building!" I growled. I would not occupy the burned-out unit again.

"But—" the contractor started.

"That's the city's problem. I'm telling you where I'm going to be and what my address is going to be. Deal with it."

I was incensed. How difficult could it be to move from one suite to another? My father owned the building; we were the tenant. The address with all our advertisements, letterheads, and paperwork would not change. The suite would.

Like the building exterior, I looked okay on the outside; but inside, I was falling to pieces. Once the nightmares began, my usual calm, fun-loving personality began to bleed away. I became testy. My language disintegrated, turning as foul as my attitude.

I started pushing builders. I pointed out things I wanted fixed, immediately. When I returned to the building a few days later, the bullet holes were still visible. Angry, I shouted f-bombs, asking why I still saw bullet holes in my building. I snarled, "When I come back, I better not see bullet holes. I don't give a shit what the subs are doing. I want those bullet holes patched. I don't want to see them again." I didn't want excuses; I wanted it my way.

As I had requested, the bushes along the street were pulled. It might not have meant anything to anyone else, but I was thankful they were gone.

* * *

In June 1986, after months of sweeping floors and flipping burgers, I began training for an assistant management position with Wendy's fast-food chain. An impressive opportunity for a twenty-year-old, I took my career path and responsibilities seriously. Along the way, I met Carol Carter, a dynamic woman with a big smile, blond hair, and a yellow mustang. We became fast friends with a similar work ethic and work style.

Following an intensive ten-week training school, we said good-bye and headed to our newly assigned restaurants—mine in Parkersburg, West Virginia, and hers just down the road in Huntington, West Virginia. The hours were long, and as new assistant managers, we often worked nights. To be effective at our jobs as managers, we also had to be strict with our employees, some of whom were from the local prison release program.

On the night of May 3, 1987, I reconciled the daily numbers, opened the round-shaped floor safe to deposit the cash, and went home to my wife. Carol worked the same shift and did the same activities. Carol Carter, however, never made it home. An employee beat her to death for the night's remittance.

I was deeply saddened by Carol's death. My entry into running a business included the brutal murder of a colleague and friend. The entire company went crazy. We cut down bushes and anything else that would stop somebody from seeing inside the store. This, however, didn't make a lot of sense because the attack happened in a small windowless 4'x4' room.

A few months later, the store closed. A once-thriving business was shuttered because of horrifying circumstances. At one point, I started to change. I sat in restaurants or public places or even at my desk and angled my back toward the corner, always on alert. I didn't want to be boxed in. If danger was lurking, I could get out to protect somebody else, to stop evildoers in their tracks, and I could do it quickly.

I became vigilant of my family and my team. I did not shy away from challenges, and I would fight to keep those I loved safe. When I moved to Florida from West Virginia, I brought the same attitude with me.

* * *

With each new hire, Headley Insurance had mandatory safety training. We also had safety meetings. All our employees knew where the fire exits were, escape routes, emergency codes, and so forth.

In 2008, it was drilled into everybody's head that no one comes in through the back door, including me. I would bang on the door in the morning and holler, "Let me in!"

Casually, the employees inside would insist, "Go around to the front."

"But I have the police with me."

"Go around front."

"I own this place."

"Too bad. Use the front door."

One day, as one of the employees unlocked the back door, I snuck up behind her as she let herself into the building. She stepped through the entryway and turned off the alarm. Her arms were filled with Christmas gifts. She seemed to be distracted because she didn't notice me. I grabbed her around the neck and whispered, "I have a gun to your head. What are you going to do?"

In less than a second, she whipped the box in her hand backward and hit me where the sun doesn't shine. Bending down, holding my privates, I rhetorically asked through gritted teeth, "What did you do?"

Not even turning to look at me, she said, "It was effective, wasn't it?" and casually walked away.

*   *   *

I would consider myself a typical man. If someone has a problem, I want to fix it—but some problems can't be fixed. If a tire is flat, I'll get out of the car and change it. People aren't tires, and they can't be replaced. That was my biggest difficulty. The files could be replaced, but Ivanna and Julieta couldn't.

In addition to increasing our security training, I could fix our payment policy. It had been our practice to allow customers to pay in cash. After the robbery, our policy changed. Burglary was not a risk I was willing to take. I began talking to other insurance agents in the area. I visited one agent, just three doors down from our address. I begged. I pleaded with him to change his policy too. "Nah, Scott"—he smiled—"lightning doesn't strike twice." Three months later, his agency was robbed at gunpoint. There were no deaths, no gunshots. I didn't even say, "I told you so." I simply bowed my head in prayer and thought, *Never again.*

Shortly thereafter, one of my customers picked her way around the construction crew and came into our temporary office. By this time, we had replaced the old RV with a work trailer.

"I'd like to make my payment," she said as she pulled a wad of bills from her wallet.

"I'm sorry, ma'am," I offered. "We are no longer taking cash."

Her eyes narrowed, and she scowled at me. "It's the law. You have to take cash."

"I'm not taking cash." I turned and pointed to the structure fifteen feet away. The building still smelled of smoke to me. I was surprised she couldn't catch a whiff of it.

She huffed and threw her statement, dollars, and change onto the desk. "You have to," she repeated. "It's the law."

"Then put me in jail. I'm not taking cash. Yours or anybody else's."

"This isn't a good business practice."

A knot formed in the back of my neck. She belittled the fact Ivanna and Julieta were dead because of a robbery. I could feel my anger rising. "Here's what you are going to do. You are going to take your business elsewhere. I don't want to lose it, but it's the way it's going to be."

"Then I want the name of another Nationwide agent right now."

"Okay." I offered her Dave Dershimer's address, the owner of the recently returned RV.

"Fine!" she shouted as she slammed the door behind her.

I looked up at Ben, who had witnessed the exchange. "You know, Dave doesn't take cash anymore either."

I shrugged. No amount of business was worth cash to me anymore.

A little later, Will Earnhardt, my Nationwide litigation specialist, called me again. The prosecutors moved forward with the criminal trial. The office rebuild pressed onward. I didn't hold my breath waiting to be served for a civil case because one wasn't coming, and I reassured Will of that fact.

*   *   *

"We can't change the office address, Scott," my contractor said, again, referring to my insistence we would change suites but not addresses.

"We will."

"It's not feasible. You'll have to get approval from everybody."

"Who's everybody?"

"The Lake Wales PD, Lake Wales FD, the US Postal Service. You have to go to a city planning meeting, get a petition, have all your neighbors sign it. Present it to the city council."

"Too fucking bad. We are moving. I don't care." If I had been an ape, I would have been beating my chest and throwing feces.

*   *   *

"Ben, come here," I insisted as I stepped over rubble in front of the building.

Ben took the lead on the restoration. He spent his days working with the construction crew, painters, and landscapers as well as working with customers who stopped by for a chat or had questions about their policies. While the building was closed, Headley customers were greeted with warmth at our temporary trailer.

Ben was the face of Headley–Lake Wales, but I snapped the orders, and what I said became the last word.

"Ben, are you carrying?"

"I've got a gun in my truck."

"That's no good. Bring your gun. Don't put it in your truck. Don't put it in your shirt. Put it on your side."

I had begun to mistrust strangers and was convinced more danger lurked in the future. Florida has generous gun regulations. While there is a concealed-weapon licenses available for both residents and nonresidents, Florida also supports a "no duty to retreat" doctrine. On private property, the weapon does not need to be concealed. And a person has the right to defend himself or herself when faced with a deadly threat. So I adopted a "no duty to retreat" attitude. I believed evil happened on December 13, and I was scared. But I was determined to rebuild and replace the damage done by Davis with justice for the girls. My first course of action: make sure someone on the property was packing heat.

"Ben, if anybody wants to come back, we've got a little something for them." From that point forward, Ben walked around the construction site with a gun on his hip.

The real reason for my paranoia was Leon Davis, who was in jail without bond. He worked alone, not part of a gang. I came across a news article that said Davis fired his counsel and would be defending himself. A few days later, the state appointed him new lawyers. My heart quickened at the sight of his name.

After the bushes were torn out, a city inspector stopped by. Lake Wales, like other central Florida cities, has a historic district that is regulated for uniformity and preservation. West Central Avenue, the street the office is on, is in the historic district and requires shrubs between the street and the sidewalk; it is code.

"Mr. Headley," the inspector said, "you're going to have to put up some shrubbery."

"No, we're not. We are putting in grass."

"Well, the problem is, you can't do that."

"Well, the problem is," I snarled, "you just watch me!"

Later, somebody else from the city called, and I let my temper fly. "Listen here, you asshole, I'm the one who just had employees burned to death. My associates are gone because of those damn bushes, and I am not putting another one back on my property. By the way, fix your stinking drainage ditch."

I was so ugly, so mean, so horrible. But they didn't make me add bushes; they even fixed the drainage ditch. The guy from the city wasn't the asshole; I was. I would have punched me in the face if I were somebody else.

* * *

I sat on the bed of my pickup truck, looking at paint samples and comparing them to the stone in the building. I held a paint chip up, squinted, and switched to another chip.

"I want this color."

"Scott, do you think maybe we could talk to somebody else about the color for the building?" one of the contractors asked.

"This one. Here." My cheeks flushed with insistence.

"Um, Scott?" he stammered. "Are you sure you want to be picking out the paint color?"

"Why the hell wouldn't I want to pick the paint color?"

"Because you're color-blind?" His voice was small, as if he were regretful of speaking the truth.

"I may be color-blind, but I can still fucking tell shades that match." No one else questioned my decision. The Hulk was a nice, mild-mannered guy, then he'd tear stuff up. That was me.

I never had a reality check with myself. I never debated my own decisions. I said, "Do it," and it was done. I would drive away thinking, *What the hell is wrong with these people?* Everybody knew I'd probably turn Hulk green in a minute—just like the Marvel comic book character—so they never allowed me to get that angry.

I was not only angry at people, I was angry at everything, including our $4,000 copier. It had significant soot and ash damage. We hired a restoration company to refurbish it. I walked in, and I unloaded my frustration on them.

"Get it out of here!" I shouted. "You can't clean it. You can't make it stop smelling of smoke. I'm tired of smelling fucking smoke. Get it out of my building. Now!"

The smell of smoke followed me everywhere. I would go to the location where we stored and sorted files. I saw nothing but blood and smelled nothing but smoke. It never seemed to end.

Before my life was upended, I relished Saturday mornings. I'd open the smoker, throw on some seasoned meat, and plan my day around applewood, peachwood, or cherry, hickory, or oak, maybe even mesquite. It was my preferred pastime. If I closed my eyes, I could almost taste the rich, sweet wood as its aroma lifted to the sky. Smoking and grilling wasn't about the meat, it was about the ritual. It was about creating savory flavors and watching others enjoy what I had prepared for them.

But food lost its flavor, and the smell of smoke made me sick. The less I slept, the more I drank. Guilt became a comfortable shoe. It was the first thing I put on in the morning and the last thing I took off at night—if I slept at all.

Before my life was upended, after enjoying a thick, rich piece of meat, I'd sit around a campfire outside my home with family and friends, sip an ice-cold beer, and smoke a fine cigar until late in the evening. It was a simple pleasure, one that wasn't extravagant but nonetheless fulfilling. But survivor's guilt replaced enjoyment. If something was satisfying in my life, it meant Ivanna and Julieta had nothing. Anything good became bad.

And anything involving smoke was sickening. The first time I vomited was at the fire. When I went to inspect the burned-out building the next day, I regurgitated again. It might have been a reaction to the smoke at the scene. It might have been triggered by the violence of the crime. Either way, the smell of smoke made me puke.

I had been a smoker, and I smoked a cigarette when I stood outside the yellow tape on West Central Avenue. But that habit rapidly disappeared. My reaction to smoke became so visceral that if I imagined smoke, I retched.

Vomit mixed with guilt interfered with my desire to cook outside, enjoy a steak, or even take pleasure in my friendships. Life became very difficult, and my anxiety mounted. I opened the garage door and looked at the four-wheelers I had stashed in the corner. They winked at me, offering me a sardonic smile. I closed the door and walked away. Inanimate objects taunted me, reminded me of the fun I used to have. Instead of remembering what my life was like before, I placed an ad in the paper and sold them along with my boat—cheap.

I didn't want to be anywhere; I didn't want to go anywhere. I wanted to hide in anonymity. I wanted to stop wearing my Headley Insurance shirts. I thought about shaving my mustache. But those are some things that made me me, and I didn't want to change—any more than they already had—for a murderer. I just wanted things to return to the way they were.

I went to the hardware store to pick up a laundry list of basics we needed, which were destroyed in the fire: brooms, mops, dust pans, and a gas-powered blower. It was an everyday type of task I craved.

* * *

The store, two blocks from the office, was a typical ma-and-pa shop, small but packed with everything. On the side was a mural of a local lake, palm trees, and wildlife. It was part of the charm of Lake Wales.

I found the broom and dust pan and blower without any difficulty. But I had to buy a gas can. With a cartful of items, I stared at the gas can. To anybody else, a gas can would just be a gas can. To me it was a big red symbol of death. With sweat on my brow, I mustered the courage and confronted the gas can.

It seemed silly. My rational side told me to pick up the can and get on with it. But I was not listening to my rational side. I was turning into an emotional wreck, fearful of inanimate objects, fearful I would be endorsing the fire, the crime, and the murders. Logic finally prevailed. I picked up the can and loaded it into my cart.

In the small town of Lake Wales, on a typical day, there are only two or three customers in the hardware store at any given time. On a busy day, there might be five at once. On this day, fifteen people were there. I hoped if I waited, everyone would pay for their purchases, and I would be alone in the store. But nobody moved toward the register. Once I finally decided to get in line, everybody else lined up behind me. We all decided to leave at once, as if the crowd could sense my weakness and life now depended on survival of the fittest.

The cashier rang up everything, and then he looked at me and laughed, "Oh, Mr. Headley, do you think it's appropriate you carry one of these around town?" He held the gas can up and shook it. "How about I just put it in a bag for you so nobody sees it?"

I didn't know what to say. I was taken off guard, shocked, and humiliated. I had confronted the gas can in the aisle, silently, privately. Now I was confronted by it again, this time, publicly, with fifteen people behind me and a jokester waving it over his head. It was a purely emotional response on my part, not a Darwinian answer to my personal struggles, but I was mortified.

Defeated, I shuffled to my truck. After loading it, I sat in the parking lot and cried. It might have only been a simple a gas can, but to me, it was a deadly weapon. When I arrived back at the office, Ben asked me if everything was okay. He could tell, immediately, I was upset.

"What's eating at you, Scott?"

"Nothing."

"Did something happen?"

"No, I'm fine."

"Scott, I need to know what happened."

I told him what transpired at the hardware store. Ben listened and went outside, I thought, so he wouldn't have to watch me cry. Again. So I wouldn't have to be embarrassed to cry in front of him. Again. I regained my composure and started to work.

About twenty minutes later, I noticed him pulling back into the parking lot. I hadn't realized he'd left.

"I took care of that," he announced as he pulled the door closed.

"Took care of what?"

"I took care of the hardware problem."

"Ben, what did you do?"

"I didn't do anything."

"What'd you do, Ben?"

Just as Ben knew something had troubled me, I knew Ben well enough to know he'd been up to something.

"I visited the store and asked, 'Which one of you assholes just waited on Mr. Headley?' A guy slowly raised his hand, and I calmly walked towards him and quietly said, 'I don't ever want to hear you ever say something so inconsiderate again.' He trembled and apologized. So I took care of that."

I shook my head and went back to work. On the face of it, I was glad Ben was on my side. He watched over me. But with each battle of mine that somebody else faced, I slipped a little bit further from myself.

Because of Leon Davis, I lost faith in my ability to protect those around me, and I began to lose faith in myself. I decided, long before construction finished, we would have a soft reopening. No grand-reopening signs. No balloons. No cookies and cake. The storefront would be closed, then it would be open. Maybe. And just as I envisioned, the office was closed, then it was ready to open.

Through all my tantrums and foot stomping, the city allowed Headley to switch sides and keep our original address. In the end, it just seemed to happen. I believe that the Lake Wales city council either felt sorry for me or didn't want to deal with the horrifying details that put their little town on the map.

Once the construction finished, I pulled aside the contractor. "The building looks phenomenal," I said with heartfelt thanks. I'd been a bear to work with, and I knew it. But I tried to be kind and offered my gratitude.

The office did look beautiful. It was furnished with built-in soft blond oak desks with black raised side panels, taupe walls and white trim, a sand-colored tile floor, and a comfortable lobby to welcome guests and clients alike. The girls would have loved it. In my mind, Ivanna made a fiesta for the customers. The aroma of homemade tamales, flautas, and chips and salsa would replace the new carpet and fresh paint smell. There would be blooming flowers on the table and sweets, which would last for days. We'd invite the entire Lake Wales community. While her laughter filled the space in my head, tears filled my eyes. The doors stayed locked.

Life went on as usual for the rest of the world, but not for me.

My wife cajoled, "The girls would be proud of what you've accomplished."

I didn't want the reopening to erase their memories. I looked at our Resolve, Courage, Hope sign proudly displayed out front surrounded by recently planted sod.

"What if nobody comes?" I asked.

"Then nobody comes."

"This place is shrouded in evil."

"We're ready to reopen. Justice will win."

Along with the rebuild in Lake Wales, my wife had begun to put up walls. We were becoming roommate instead of lovers. There was the occasional hug or peck on the cheek. But her counsel was important to me. I looked out the window. A police cruiser drove past. I prayed to God my wife was right.

CRUMBLING CASTLES

The irritability I experienced during the restoration turned to fury. I bottled up every emotion. It became my mission to protect everyone around me from the horrors of my experience, the drama surrounding the criminal trial, and the continual terrors I dreamed every night.

I was furious for several reasons. Surviving tragedy, being left to pick up the pieces is heartbreaking. My employees were nice people who radiated love and joy in everything they did. My helplessness to stop the attack weighed on me, but I didn't tell anybody; instead, I lashed out at those around me.

For relief, I started to visit the gym just to throw something heavy around—barbells, hand weights, a punching bag. When I worked out, my brain stopped. Shock, distress, and grief disappeared with each repetition. Nobody at the gym knew my agony. Nobody there saw my emptiness. I just looked like every other gym rat punishing himself. It became my place of refuge.

I didn't mind the small talk: "How many sets do you have left?" or "What's your max?" If somebody needed a spotter for a bench press, a simple nod with eye contact would suffice. Nobody needed to say a word, and help would appear.

Fully immersed in my workout, the rest of the world vanished. As my nights got longer and more sleepless, my workouts became more ferocious. I was a forty-year-old man with a six-pack and almost no body fat. To the rest of the gym, I looked thin and trim. To me, I looked gaunt and ghastly.

Each ripple, each defined muscle represented a scar. There was no joy in my physique. Rather, each workout fueled my need for chastisement—and exhaustion. If I could be tired enough, I might sleep. If the workout lasted long enough, I might break and experience relief. But relief was elusive. So I pushed harder, engaged in small talk, and avoided my memories.

But not always.

"Hey, you're Scott Headley."

"Yeah."

I pulled a dead lift.

"Dude, I'm really sorry about what happened."

I set the bar down.

"Thanks." I followed the small talk script.

I pulled a dead lift again.

"You've got to tell me what happened."

I set the bar down.

"Nah."

I lifted the weights again and set them down.

"Yeah, man, I get it. Okay," he said.

The gym was busy. Televisions flashed a variety of channels to entertain people on treadmills or stair climbers. Gym goers wandered from one machine to another. Some laid mats on the floor for sit-ups and push-ups. Heavy metal music played in the background to push the flow of adrenaline.

He didn't go away. He followed me to the dumbbells. "Scott, man, I gotta know."

I stopped, sat on a bench, and waited for him to sit on the bench across from me. I spoke matter-of-factly. "He entered the building with a can of gasoline, a lighter, duct tape, and a gun . . ." I spit the words out, as if they were as hot as the fire Davis lit. It was a line I couldn't say without vehemence. I watched the gym rat's face. The idea he'd have a ringside seat to a horror movie quickly faded as I immersed him into the pain of real life. In the midst of grief, there is relief in the sharing. That's what the shrinks all say. And there was an odd liberation when I could unload my story onto a stranger—unfair as it might have been. The color slowly left his cheeks. I finished my report, grabbed my towel, and headed to the locker room. He stayed on the bench, stunned. I left drained of energy.

That night, I dreamed in the color of blood. A stranger walked into a two-story building. I stood looking out the second-floor window when men in dark masks, carrying guns and knives, followed the stranger through the door. I rushed to the stairs and crept toward the lower level. A stair creaked; the masked men turned toward me. I yelled, but no sound came from my mouth. The man sat on a bench, not moving from his place. I wanted to help him, to save him. He seemed content to watch.

I awoke in a pool of sweat, panting, unable to escape. I my closed eyes and drifted back to blackness. Along with my sweat, I couldn't breathe; air, it seemed, was as elusive as a restful night.

* * *

In the morning, I wiped moisture from the bathroom mirror and looked at my skeletal frame. As the steam faded, the circles under my eyes captured my attention; they looked vacant. My eyes wandered to my torso, and I studied my emotional scars represented by my muscles. They were adorned by several tattoos I'd received over the years.

Each tattoo was designed by me to remind me of something. On my left shoulder is an image of the good Lord's hands, together in prayer, surrounded by the cloudy heavens. The hands are a replica of my son's hands, skillfully drawn, humbly worn. In the mix is a skylark.

Before my mom's death, everyone called her Skylark. She had an online ministry where she prayed for handicapped people, people who couldn't make it to church. The skylark sits above my heart and looks toward the sky, hopeful and always alert.

My right pec looks like a bear claw ripped my chest open. Behind it is the American flag. When I watched the Twin Towers fall, I was scared. Was this going to happen everywhere? Would they come after all of us? I did not want to travel; I did not want to get onto a plane. "They are coming back. They are coming back to finish it."

I felt like a voyeur as I watched first responders run into burning buildings from the comfort of my living room. They dug for hours looking for survivors. They carried both the living and the dead, covered in ash so thick it made the entire city gray. Those were my heroes, the selfless men and women who thought of others first. They are what America is all about. And I proudly wear my flag on my chest to stand with them. In September 2001, I asked myself, had NYC been my city, would I have been as courageous? I hoped I would be.

I thought about Julieta and Ivanna. Time had done little to extinguish my anguish. I studied my tattoos, meant to remind me of God's watchful eye. I wanted to hang my head in shame because I have replaced my reverence for God with wrath for Leon Davis. Instead, I touched my flag. I traced the claw marks with my fingers. Tingling chills climbed through my chest as I reminded myself America came back from 9/11. It was painful. It scared everybody. But we united and rebuilt.

* * *

We reopened the Lake Wales office with the same American spirit. My fears that it might erase the girls' memories were unfounded. My wife was right; the girls would have been proud.

The first customer through the door was a firefighter. He had been at the scene. He might have stood on our roof. "I'm glad you decided to reopen your office."

I smiled and shook his hand. It was a simple gesture, proof that due process might succeed. Shortly thereafter, a deputy sheriff walked through the door, and a few days later, another firefighter. Within a month, it seemed like every first responder in the area had come to Headley, to support us, to stand strong with us. To each customer, I gave a US flag pin. It was something we'd done for thirty years. It was something I was proud to do again.

The United States is a country founded upon principle. The right to pursue happiness. The right to tranquility and prosperity. The right to gun ownership. I have collected guns most of my adult life. My personal favorite is a .38 Special. There is a certain comfort knowing it is near. While I've never had to use it to defend myself against another man, there was a time, when my son and I were walking around the lake near our home, when we stepped too closely to an alligator's nest. The mama gator, who stood watchfully nearby, charged us. I drew my weapon, cocked the pistol, and pointed. The mother stopped and stared at me, my other arm pushing my son behind me. She must have known the sound. She heard the click and, after a split second, turned and dove into the murky water.

My gun may give me a false sense of security, but I feel protected just the same. After the robbery, I decided I wanted to have one on me at all times.

My next tattoo, a .38 Special, was painted onto my chest in honor of Ivanna and Julieta. On top of the barrel sits my skylark, calmly watching the gunfire and the smoke bellow into the clouds that were already there. Over the barrel reads a banner: Never Again.

*   *   *

Things began to return to normal for everyone but me. I'd been forced into limbo; I was left with terrifying nightmares and a phobia of fueling stations. In the quest for balance, I ordered a custom part for my truck at a local shop. It buoyed my mood to know it was ready to be picked up.

It was difficult to imagine a simple air intake system for my Nismo could bring me happiness, but sometimes a little retail therapy is a good thing. Conveniently, the store was adjacent to a restaurant, and I stopped there first.

It was lunchtime, and the narrow but long eatery was crowded. "There's a wait right now," the host said without looking up from the seating chart.

"I can see you are busy. Can I order to go?"

"Sure." She tipped her head toward the back of the restaurant and pointed to the To Go sign and then looked at me. "If you go to the back, someone can take your order." She handed me a menu. "I'll show you."

I followed her through the '50s-style diner. The sparkly red vinyl booths along the wall were filled with mechanics and bankers alike. The matching barstools on the other side were full as well; some patrons were in a hurry, and some looked like they'd been there awhile. I smiled at a soldier sitting in a booth by himself and instinctively put my hand over the flag tattooed on my chest.

"I'd like a burger, all the way, fries, and a cola," I announced to the person at the register.

"No problem. It will be ready in twenty minutes. You can wait here if you'd like."

"And the guy over there, by the window in the army uniform, put this towards his meal." I handed him an extra twenty-dollar bill. "I'll be right back." I smiled and practically bounced out of the restaurant with the knowledge I was heading to a candy store for truck enthusiasts.

Cargo containment systems, custom rims, do-it-yourself window tinting; aftermarket running boards, alarms, and a million types of truck toolboxes—the store was filled from top to bottom with state-of-the-art truck parts.

I milled around, picking up one item then another until the twenty minutes was almost up. With my purchased piece in hand, I returned to pick up my meal. A jangle of the door chime announced my arrival while I pushed my glasses to the top of head.

A woman waiting to be seated smiled when she saw me. "Excuse me, are you Mr. Headley?"

I glanced at my shirt, monogrammed with Headley Insurance, and smiled. "Yes, ma'am, I am."

"Mr. Headley, I just wanted to tell you how sorry I am about your employees." Her Southern drawl was evident at the end of *Headley* and *employee*. She offered a sad smile, not radiant or joyful, but tucked in at the corner.

"Thank you." I gave a curt smile in reply as I placed a hand on her arm. "It means a lot to me."

And it did mean a lot. But, once again, I felt singled out. The small pleasure of picking up a truck part was replaced by grief. I lowered my head in an attempt to regain composure.

There was this old man in his seventies sitting at the bar, drinking beer. He craned his neck and watched as I chatted and said a simple good-bye to the woman.

"That's just fucking terrible," he slurred, spitting out the vulgar word louder than the others. "I can't believe what this world's coming to."

His comment startled me. It *was* terrible, and I felt the sting of grief at almost every moment of the day. I shook my head and continued toward the back of the restaurant.

"Don't get me wrong," he added, his loud drunken speech echoing around the diner. "I'd pay somebody to kill a couple of fucking Mexicans for me."

The entire restaurant grew quiet. I stopped. Ice ran through my veins; I counted to ten, trembled, and shook with rage.

Suddenly, I'm a fourteen-year-old boy in West Virginia, fighting my way through school. "Hey, look who it is, white trash!" I was family proud then, and I was family proud now. I took some licks as a kid, but it's not the size of the man in the fight. It's the size of the fight in the man. And right then, I was transported back to West Virginia, ready to fight.

My parents' divorce had been nasty. What was a comfortable life in Florida turned into a move to West Virginia to be near the rest of our extended family. My dad became a guy I might see once a year, and my mom decided to punish him by renting a small home the size of a two-car garage on the wrong side of the tracks and accepting the $135 child support Dad paid instead of going to court to fight for more. Regardless, we worked hard and made do with little.

Most of the kids I knew lived on the other side of town, about five blocks away. They wore expensive jeans and top-of-the-line sneakers; I wore the best discount stores had to offer. When I was a teenager, I saved up some money and bought a secondhand bike. Another kid watched as I polished and fussed over it.

"That's one sweet bike," he mused as he ran his hand over the frame.

"Yeah, I know."

"Can I borrow it?"

"No, you'll mess it up."

"Come on, Scott."

"Not today, it's new."

"It's not new. It's a secondhand bike."

"It's new to me."

He lived in a nice home, with upscale parents who had high social expectations and disapproving stares. He let his entitlement carry over to the playground and did as he pleased.

One day I saw him riding a bike just like mine. When I arrived home, mine was missing.

"Dude," I said when I called him. "You can't just walk into my home when nobody's here and take what you want."

"Scott, man, what's the big deal?"

"I just saw you riding around on my bike. The big deal is, your parents would throw me in jail if I broke into your house."

"That's different," he said flippantly. "You live over there."

I lived over there. I didn't matter. The verbal punch hit my gut. He challenged me to a fight at Thirty-Ninth Street Beach, a place where there were no cops, where there were no parents. Somebody got beat up. Somebody didn't. We always had friends who separated us if it got too bad.

I accepted his challenge and walked to the end of Thirty-Ninth Street. He insulted my mom's home, my family—taking what he thought he was entitled to. He was larger than I was in every way. That didn't matter. The size of the fight in me was bigger than his.

"It's not like I need it anyway," he said as he let it fall onto the dusty gravel.

I watched the stones scatter and met him nose to nose. I clenched my fist. I stepped back. He started to walk forward.

"It's just a crappy b—"

He didn't finish his sentence. I swung and heard my fist connect with his face. There was a sudden gush of blood; he clenched his nose as he fell. The fight was over. I rode my bike home, proudly.

And like my bike, I was proud of Ivanna and Julieta. I made a fist and unrolled it slowly, stretching my fingers in an attempt to remain calm. I walked up to the man on the stool and stood an inch from his nose. He smelled of sweat and day-old booze. I would not be shamed by a seventy-something-year-old man.

"Hey, asshole," I said with a low, even voice, "my girls were Mexican."

Forks scraped. Ice rattled in glasses. Nobody spoke. I turned and smoothly walked to the back of the diner. The server recognized me and handed me my to-go bag. I don't remember if he even charged me, but I do remember the long walk to the front door. The door chime signaled my exit.

*   *   *

I returned to the office fighting mad, horrified someone could be so rude, angry I'd be singled out, and upset my life revolved around such a horrendous story. I pushed papers across my desk mumbling swear words. As the criminal trial ramped up, Davis's name was in every newscast, which meant mine was too, along with a photo of me from the fire.

A few days after the diner incident, Ben and I ventured out to lunch together. Walking into a small Cuban café, I pushed my glasses to the top of my head and scooted into a booth. A woman sitting at a table nearby quickly put her menu over her mouth.

"That's the guy whose employees were killed," she whispered to her companion. It was soft, but in a small restaurant, sound travels as much as the smell of the fried plantains being delivered to the table behind ours.

Her companion leaned over, made a pointing motion meant to be hidden by her hand, and replied, "Oh, that was just awful. That poor, poor man. Bless his heart."

I looked at Ben and said, "Do they really think I can't figure out what they are saying?"

"Yup. Maybe it's your glasses. Maybe you should leave them in your truck."

"You think?"

"When they are perched on top of your head, you look just like your photo from the fire. And the funeral. And the vigil. And the news."

"Yeah, maybe. I guess. I'm wearing the Headley shirt too."

"Hey, lots of us wear the shirt. Your glasses on top of your head is your thing. If you didn't have them on, maybe people wouldn't recognize you so quickly."

"I'll try it. Good point."

As the women left, the waitress started to clear their table. I could see they had only left change for her gratuity. I watched as she picked up the meager tip and whispered a prayer and made the sign of a cross. She slid a nickel into her hand, which had fallen off the check-holder tray. I was amazed she could be appreciative of so little.

"Here you go," she said as she set our sandwiches onto the table a little bit later. "You gentlemen, enjoy your lunch."

Her demeanor was joyous, her chin high. I wondered how someone who seemed to be okay with receiving such a paltry tip could have such a bright spirit. "You're a happy person, aren't you?" I rhetorically commented when she asked if she could bring us anything else.

"I'm grateful for everything I have. Really, I'm blessed."

After we paid for our meal, I threw an extra $50 bill onto the table as a thank-you for reminding me of the gratefulness in some people.

* * *

The thing I didn't want to happen happened. I changed because the events on December 13, 2007, made me. I stopped wearing my signature glasses—in public, and it helped. The number of times I was recognized went down. I walked into restaurants as Scott, not as "the guy whose employees were killed," which was a relief. But I didn't just change on the outside; I changed on the inside too. I had become irritable and tense and paranoid. And I relived the trauma through night terrors.

There's a difference between nightmares and night terrors. Something else I didn't know but was beginning to learn. Nightmares are painful distortions of the subconscious, anxiety producing, sleep disrupting. I had several nightmares after the robbery, as if, in my subconscious, I could fix the past. Maybe, with enough practice, I could restore my life to the way it was before. As if I were attempting to change the horrifying truth—even though each dream scenario involved strange people in strange locations. As time moved on, I feared going to sleep. The more afraid I became, the more fretful I acted, drinking more alcohol, postponing sleep time, behaving erratically. The dreams drained me. My initial sleep pattern after the robbery, which cycled around predictable (although scary) dreams, slowly changed.

Almost eighteen months after the deaths of Ivanna and Julieta, I would awaken wet with sweat, my linens soaked, tossed, and tangled. I started sleepwalking. One night, in the heat of battle, I crept from my covers and crawled from the bedroom to the railing at the top of the stairs. Blankets, draped from the banister for a spring-cleaning air-out, provided cover from the enemy. I rose, fired my imaginary weapon, then crouched again. The blankets entangled my foot, and I fought, wrestling them to the ground before flinging them and me over the barrier to the landing nineteen stairs below. I was confused, screaming, and not quite aware of my surroundings. Sleep became a dangerous sporting event that left me bruised and battered—me against my subconscious. And my subconscious was winning. I worried I would hurt my wife with my flailing arms and legs, and I made the decision to move to the guest bedroom.

I had become a porcupine with a coat of quills. It was for the safety of my wife I moved to the guest bedroom, and it was my loss. Moving to the guest suite was the right choice, but it did nothing for my marriage. My crabby attitude spilled into my family life. My wife went about her days productive and astute to the needs of others. The way she always had been. We married young, had three children together, and now, we both grieved for the loss of women we had grown to love. She was understanding of my grief, even solicitous, but she put up barriers to protect herself from my arrogant, often biting remarks. I pushed the limits of our vows "to have and to hold, in good times and bad" to extremes.

Our family conversations focused on business rather than on ordinary living. I would become irritated if the kids had problems: woe is me—my windshield wipers need replacing. I couldn't understand how they could be so selfish when Julieta and Ivanna were *dead*. My self-centeredness created a rift that robbed my family of a father and husband.

My nights alone were more like a workout than a peaceful interlude. It was like running a ten-mile race. I would rouse terrified and exhausted, out of breath, and drenched. Fall back to sleep and run those ten miles again. The truth is, I was terrified and exhausted about what was happening outside of work. In desperation, I visited my doctor and confessed my concerns. My dreams had turned into night terrors. Night terrors, he explained, occur during deeper sleep. They create an abstract reaction—an awakened yet undesired response. Alcohol often increases night terrors. I had to make a lifestyle change for the sake of my productivity, my marriage, my life. My doctor also recommended a sleep study.

Without another option, I finally went to a sleep lab. The nightstand next to the bed was oak laminate, homey, but cheap. The room didn't look like a bedroom with its sterile floors, ecru-colored walls, and intercom and camera. I arrived around 9:00 p.m. They hooked me up with wires and electrodes, some on my face and head, some on my arms, and a strap around my chest. I looked like a test subject in an alien movie.

The wires were attached to some machine above the top of the bland hospital bed. It seemed there must have been twenty or thirty of them, and I feared moving would disrupt the entire process. The whole thing felt ridiculous. I might have laughed if I saw someone else foolishly taped up like a Christmas tree, but I was the one the technicians were looking at, studying, watching. I didn't normally sleep, and I was pretty sure, with an audience and all this stuff attached to me, I wouldn't sleep now. As my thoughts wandered, the whole experience seemed a waste of time. The plastic-covered bed crackled as I lay back. The lights dimmed, and the hum of the machines haunted my ears. I tried to think of other things as I lay in the bed for what seemed an eternity until I slowly drifted off to my usual fitful sleep.

A bit later, I sensed the technician in the room and was awakened by the hushed sounds of hands against machinery. I had been asleep, but without my clock, I had no idea if it were an hour or three. She fiddled with the wires then placed a machine over my head and nose. Groggy and unsettled, I opened my eyes for a second then closed them again for more rest. I took a breath in and drifted into a deep sleep.

It was a feeling I hadn't experienced in a long time, floating comfortably, relaxed, calm.

"Excuse me, Scott?" the nurse said softly, apologetically, as she tapped my shoulder.

My eyes flashed open. I looked around the room. There was no haze in my normally tired eyes—everything was in focus, and I was alert. "What time is it?"

"It's five in the morning." She began to take the electrodes off my body. "I know you're tired and probably just want to go home and go to bed."

"Tired? Tired!" I sat up and pulled the funny contraption from my face. "I feel like a million bucks!" I'd slept three beautiful hours. I had not had such a restful sleep since December 12, 2007. I had energy, lots of energy. I might have entered the study feeling silly, but I left with relief and a smile.

On average, the doctor later told me, I had quit breathing some seventy times. Sleep apnea. My breathing was interrupted, my airway blocked by the soft tissue in the back of my throat. I woke up choking, gasping for air, sleeping only one and a half hours, night after night, month after month, for well over a year.

My night terrors were brought on by numerous things: anxiety, stress, alcohol (which I knew I had to cut back on), and improper breathing at night. The CPAP machine, the funny thing that fit over my nose, solved my breathing issues by running a slow and steady stream of air through my nose. This didn't alleviate my terrors entirely, but it helped. It helped a lot.

Gag Orders

Again, Will, the Nationwide litigation specialist, called. Leon Davis had changed defense attorneys, again. The burned-out office was now opened in its new location. But there was no news about a civil trial, and I wasn't worried.

Regardless, Will prepared me for what he thought was inevitable. I was in complete denial. Anybody would be insane to think I was the reason these girls were burned to death. I couldn't fathom any attorney taking this case.

One month later, I received discovery papers from an attorney I'd never heard of. Before I called Will, I tried to find her on the Internet. She was a small-time lawyer, and it didn't worry me. She wasn't a serious player; she didn't even make a blip on the radar.

To Will, her questions were a fishing expedition. At his suggestion, I answered her inquiries with rudimentary responses. Eventually, she faded into the sunset.

In the sunset, apparently, she met a bigger fish. Five or six months after she disappeared, I received actual suit papers for damages by the estate of Julieta's son, Baby Michael, and for personal negligence by Julieta's mother.

The new attorney, Rick Richards, began a course of civil discovery. He wanted the same types of documents and more. He asked for printouts of policies and policy limits; he requested copies of time cards for everybody who'd worked at Headley for the past eight years or so. He sought payroll reports, remittance reports, and demographic reports. And he requested a gag order.

There was so much hype around the upcoming Leon Davis criminal trial that both the media and interested outsiders wanted to know about "how it was going." People often stopped by the office to chat and would bring up the incident. Occasionally, a phone call from an interested party might ring and inquire about the case. With fear for a tainted jury pool, the judge allowed the gag order even before the criminal trial subpoenas arrived.

In my world, things like clinical depression and post-traumatic stress disorder didn't exist, until I experienced it. My heart grew numb with Richard's interrogatories. His questioning was brutal. It stirred up emotions of despair and emptiness like I had never known. Could he really believe I saw this happening in the future? That I was the reason after all?

In terms of logic, the rationale didn't work. Clearly, Richards was chasing the money, but the mind plays tricks. Richards had caught himself a big fish, and he wasn't going to let go.

Shortly thereafter, the first criminal subpoena arrived. It contained a request for documents and statements from several Headley employees. It was broad and nonspecific. I tried to be comforting and reassuring that everything was okay. At the same time, it overwhelmed me. I knew the day would come when I would see Davis in court. But more importantly, I didn't want my staff to see Davis in court. I was unsure of how to prevent this, but I hoped if I could be diligent and thorough, it would be possible.

The second subpoena arrived two days later, addressed personally to me. I accepted the subpoena, my stomach sinking, and opened it up. The document told me I could not discuss or review any information connected to the Davis trial. This gag order was more restrictive than the civil one. I could not read a newspaper, peruse an online newsroom, or ask questions of my friends and neighbors. My life was toppled by Davis in a way I couldn't have fathomed.

A third subpoena arrived, then a fourth. By the time the fifth subpoena arrived, I smiled and said hello to the person delivering it. What else could I do? She was the same deputy sheriff who had delivered the first four folded, signed, and stamped notes. She was the same deputy who delivered the civil suit subpoena. This time, she had come to deliver a subpoena to another member of my team. Within a week, the entire office was on a first-name basis with the woman in the green uniform. Each subpoena came with a start date and an end date. Each time the trial dates changed, so would the subpoenas. It was agony—like being called to the principal's office and not knowing when you're going to see him or even what it might be about.

Living under a gag order stifled my relationships and refused me the council of friends and colleagues. Acquaintances would see me at work, in the gym, or in the dairy aisle at the local supermarket. They engaged me in conversation.

"Hey, Scott," someone in the grocery store would say. "It's good to see you." They would smile and stop their cart. If it were a woman, she'd offer me a light hug, whereas a man would offer his right hand to shake and a left hand on my shoulder to provide comfort. We'd make small talk until he or she would ask something like, "Do the prosecutors have enough evidence to put this bastard away?"

I'd cut them off. "Tim," or "Tammy," I'd reply, "I sure hope so. It was great seeing you. Tell your wife/husband I said hi." Then I'd continue on my path to pick up a gallon of milk or brick of cheese. It left me feeling empty. The robbery, fire, and trial became the biggest things in my life; and I couldn't talk about them—not to my friends, not to my family, not even to my wife.

"Do they have dogs that can sniff out a computer?"

"What?" a friend responded.

"You know, like bomb-sniffing dogs. Do they have dogs that can find hidden computers?"

"I don't think so. Why?"

"What about undercover subpoena officers? Somebody whose sole responsibility is to entrap people in gag orders."

"I don't think that's gonna happen."

"Hmmm. This whole thing makes me so mad."

"I know."

I finally began to see a psychologist with the hopes of gaining a grip on my life because I hadn't just slipped into a funk, I started to lose relationships. My children, for example. And my friends. And the most important person in my life, my wife.

* * *

While the criminal trial ramped up, a whole new batch of interrogatories from Richards's civil suit came in. And when I say interrogatories, I'm talking about a one-inch ream of paper typed in itty-bitty font.

I cooperated with the liability adjusters who asked for similar information. I cooperated with our attorneys, who tried to help me. I never lied or misled anybody, but I grew damn tired of cooperating with the plaintiff's attorney. I spent the majority of my time producing documentation. I couldn't escape the stress of litigation—criminal or civil. While I had a team of employees who were keeping the business afloat, I suddenly realized I worked for Richards and decided it was time to quit. I phoned my attorney.

"If he wants any more paper from me, Richards can put me on the payroll. If that asshole wants me to dig through that muck, I'll tell him what I'm worth by the hour, and he can pay me my owner's salary. And I want my first ten hours up front."

Richards didn't like that. He countered: I could pass the interrogatories on to an employee and he might consider paying one of them.

"I will not subject my employees," I responded to my attorney, "to dig through fire-ridden boxes and smoky ash and filth." I started shouting, "*He* suggests I am the reason the girls are dead, and now *he* wants my employees to work for him! If that asshole wants the information, it will be produced by me at my hourly rate."

You Did It, Admit It

News of the criminal trial trickled in. I might not have been allowed to talk about it, but it didn't mean I couldn't become a good listener. Scuttlebutt around the office, news channels in the gym, and the occasional visit from lawyers filled me in on details without the fear of computer-sniffing dogs.

Andrew and Rachel Nolin had been appointed as Davis's attorneys. I had never heard of them, nor did I care who they were. I was tired of living in fear and ready to move on. At first, Davis refused to have a jury trial. Then his attorneys threatened to quit. Next, he changed his mind again, and jury selection began on July 12, 2010. By July 14, the entire jury pool was dismissed. According to papers, an issue arose regarding the defense's use of an expert who could discuss the reliability of eyewitnesses. It was an issue that might have been important, but to me, it just extended the ordeal by three months.

In October 2010, Paul Wallace, the prosecutor, asked me to meet him at the Lake Wales office after hours one night. He wanted to prepare me for what I might see, hear, and be asked as a witness. He discussed my business practices and safety policies. He asked me questions about Davis and about my whereabouts at the time of the fire.

"Do you know Leon Davis?"

"Only what I read in the papers."

"Do you know why Davis would rob the office?"

"No."

"Were your fire alarms working? Did you have an emergency policy in place? How do you handle disgruntled customers?"

I had been looking toward finding justice for my colleagues, hoping to put the nightmares behind me, but Wallace showed me pictures, which brought back memories I had worked hard to bury. The crime scene photos evoked the stench of wet drywall and burnt flesh. The things in my nightmares came to life on the table in front of me. Photos from the hospital of Baby Michael, eyes sealed shut, barely the size of the palm he was lying in. Photos of Ivanna, her red-raw skin, swollen and peeling, her fingers charred black. Photos of Julieta, her hand with missing fingernails, covered in red, white, and black tissue. Photos I had not seen and now could not unsee.

Wallace asked some additional questions. I answered each query honestly. I knew I didn't have ESP, but with each answer, I questioned myself, *Why didn't I know Davis would inflict such awful pain?* It was the not knowing that continued to cause me turmoil.

After he left, I went outside and retched.

*   *   *

The first morning I had been subpoenaed to be in the courtroom filled me with angst. My biggest fear would be seeing Leon Davis. To metaphorically say he took up residency in my mind would be an understatement. Even though I might not have seen him in my dreams, he was the reason for my nightmares, and I feared my reaction to him. Would the angry Scott snap, or would it be the numb, detached one?

I arrived before the appointed time of 8:00 a.m. The DA directed me to a sitting area outside the courtroom—the witness room. It was a small chamber attached to the courtroom, designed for hostile and high-profile witnesses alike. The place wasn't cozy. Somebody, sometime, tried to create a professional seating area. It had burgundy or maybe blue padded seats with chrome arms, a small wooden table, and overhead industrial lighting.

"The bailiff will come and tell you when it's your turn," he instructed. "Just sit tight. It will all be over soon."

I pursed my lips and nodded as if I understood. I didn't, really. I was nervous and scared and wished I could crawl back in bed to hide my fear that justice might not prevail.

"Mr. Headley, Scott?" another attorney said.

"Yes, sir." I stood and stretched my neck to the side.

"We're not going to need you today."

I glanced at my watch—ten thirty-five. I gathered my magazines and strode from the seating area to the elevators, attempting to look relaxed and laid-back. Several people from the media milled around, hoping to collect statements from both witnesses and lawyers.

I was a key witness, employer of Ivanna and Julieta. Owner of the company that was robbed and torched. I'm sure they would have loved to take my statement. It was the media, after all, who splashed my photo on front-page news and claimed I was assessing my building. Their behavior, in my eyes, was deplorable. But I had put on airs, as if I weren't bothered by the prospect of returning to court, hoping my act was believable regardless of the fact I was bound and gagged and frustrated and scared.

The second time, I waited in the witness room for hours. It was the fifth day of the trial, and this time, I wasn't alone. Sitting opposite me were two other witnesses—an older woman and a thirtysomething man. I assumed they were Leon Davis's family because I didn't recognize them. We were the only people in the little room, which was what I began to call it. It was an awkward affair sitting opposite defense witnesses, wondering what they would be asked and how they might answer. What did they know? Did they know why Leon had behaved so cruelly? Did they believe I was the reason for Leon's actions? They had nothing to do but glower. Their glaring alarmed me. I was powerless against it, tense, unsure, and worried. I wondered how they could know such a monster and not do anything to stop him.

They stared at me the entire time; I tried to act like sitting in a rundown room was nothing. I was a busy man. I had people to see, places to be, things to do. I pretended to answer an e-mail or two. I spoke softly into the phone and made it look like I was working. But sitting there, avoiding the hostility seeping across the seating area by the defense witnesses, I couldn't concentrate on anything. I was dog-tired from nightmares and exercise, and I was ready to hurry the trial along.

A few hours later, another attorney sent me home. I went to the office and worked as if things were ordinary, or as ordinary as they could be, calling clients, working on spreadsheets. One of my agents suddenly stopped and made a funny face. Not funny ha-ha; rather, she skewed her nose and contorted her mouth into this odd scrunch. "What?" I asked. We both knew she couldn't tell me anything about the trial.

She shook her head, "Nothing." She made mini crisscross signs with her hands, one over the other, about three times, then put her finger against her mouth as if to say, "Shhh, I can't tell you this."

"What can't you tell me?" It had to be about the trial.

"I'm not telling you there's been a mistrial."

"What?" I shouted. "Goddammit!"

How could there be a mistrial? My body tensed up. Years of preparation, months of gag orders and subpoenas. I couldn't take it. What did it mean? A mistrial? We would have to start all over again. Maybe my reaction was selfish. I wanted justice for the girls, and I wanted the monster to be put away, but I also wanted the trial to be behind me.

I got the full story later that day. Everybody got the story. It was the trial of the century in Central Florida, and it dominated the news. "Breaking," every news channel said. They showed the video.

It was something the witnesses for the prosecution had been prepared for, questions about the crime scene; questions about the manhunt; questions about Leon Davis; and questions that might, that could, and that should be asked.

But it was complicated.

Through all the pretrial motions, it had been determined what Julieta told the emergency crews and the people in the restaurant could not count as testimony.

In the court system, a person is innocent until proven guilty. A person charged with a crime is able to meet their accuser in court and listen, firsthand, to the other's sworn testimony. Secondhand is considered hearsay and not allowed. It contains someone else's interpretation of the statement.

Julieta's words immediately after the attack were considered inadmissible because Julieta is dead and unable to speak to the accused. Because Julieta is dead. Because evil killed her; evil was assumed innocent. Evil would not have to face his accuser, who is dead because of him. Irony.

But Ivanna's words could be used. More irony. Ivanna thought she would die when she talked with Farah Moody and waited for help. Ivanna asked Farah to pray for her because she didn't think she'd make it.

The difference between Ivanna's words and Julieta's words was negligible in life, but not in death. Julieta asked someone to pray for her baby. Ivanna asked Farah to pray for *her*, which established *her* words as a fact, not hearsay. It's called a dying declaration. Ivanna's words could be used in court without Leon Davis facing her because Ivanna thought she would die.

One of the paramedics, during his testimony, offered his account of Ivanna's words. That Leon Davis had been the one to pour gasoline on her. That Leon Davis had wrapped her with duct tape. That Leon Davis had killed her, and he added, "She raised up on the stretcher and said emphatically that Leon Davis did this."[12]

It was hearsay, the word *emphatically*. The judge immediately ordered a mistrial. The countenance of the paramedic's face fell. It had been videotaped by various news outlets. I watched in disbelief on television later in the afternoon. With a flat face, he audibly said, "Oops."

I wanted to cry for him. I wanted to cry for me. I wanted to cry for Ivanna, her words were, essentially, used against her—not Leon Davis.

The judge told the paramedic, "I have no choice but to declare a mistrial."

Instantly, a woman started shouting, "You know you did it! You know you did it!" The voice impassioned, strained, panicked. The camera panned onto Isabella Ramirez, Ivanna's mother, who stood at the edge of a courtroom seat and pointed at Leon Davis then heaved her purse toward him. Her bag hit Rachel Nolin, Davis's attorney, instead.

The cameras continued to roll. Roland Barrera, Ivanna's father, had been sitting in the second row next to his wife. He rose and dove over the bench in front of him and the low wooden panel in front of that. Less than a second after the mistrial had been declared, he'd attacked Davis. Ivanna's father had to be forcibly restrained by a sheriff's deputy. The officer pushed him against the barrier, and with cameras trained on Barrera, he cursed and brushed the front of his own arms as if wiping dirt from himself.

I watched on the television at the gym. I cursed too then worked out my aggression.

Ivanna's father, someone later told me, believed a mistrial meant the end of the ordeal—Leon Davis would be a free man. He wasn't a free man, but the dance started all over, again. Now the second jury would be excused. Next, they'd have to find a third jury, and I would have to stay bound and gagged.

Three months later, in January 2011, I sat in the same room with the same padded chairs. The same two people sat across me. This time, four sheriff's deputies joined us in the room. They were all dressed in heavy green polyester. Their sleeves adorned with the same Polk County emblem. Their heavy braided belts held a variety of holsters for a phone and pepper spray and a collapsible baton. What the belt didn't hold was obvious. The gun holsters were empty.

I sat in an uncomfortable chair, and the deputies stood with empty holsters. They became a physical wall between the Davis family and me. The officers tried to give off the vibe they were there to protect me from the media circus. Not one time did any of them make eye contact with me. They excluded me from conversation. They might have been dispassionate observers of the trial, but to me, they seemed cold and distant. Even though they were protecting me from the media—or the media from me—they acted like they were doing me a service, keeping me from potentially doing something that could land me in jail. I'm certain the Davis family would have snapped comments to me, and I would not have hesitated to have a conversation with them had it not been for the officers.

The Davises continued to stare at me through the wall of deputies. Their eyes told me they thought I was a liar. The police made false accusations about their loved one. I was a piece of crap and the reason Leon Davis was on trial.

Looking between my phone and the back of the green-clad shoulders, I thought about the whole scenario. I had always believed in the goodness of people. I knew bad things happened. It happened to Carol Carter, my colleague who was slain in West Virginia. Although Carol's death was horrible, it was a robbery for money; she was in the wrong place at the wrong time. What happened to Julieta and Ivanna was cruel beyond words.

Besides the comments I'm sure they would have made, I also questioned my own culpability. My goal had been to create successful associates, to prop each employee up until they reached the sky and achieved their dreams. I felt I personally let them down because I was powerless to stop the chain of events that led to their deaths. Logically, I knew I didn't have the power to save them, but it didn't make me feel any better. I glanced at the deputies and their empty holsters. They didn't have firepower either.

Occasionally, other witnesses joined us in the little room. I sat in the chamber with the Davises on several different occasions. It was often enough to notice they seemed to make a habit of following people into the bathroom. Once, someone followed me in. I stood by the urinal; he entered the stall and began snapping comments. "If this were a white man, this wouldn't be going on right now, but he's automatically guilty because he's black."

It felt confrontational. It felt threatening. For a split second, I panicked at my naked exposure to the world. But I had my hackles up, ready to fight four or five men. I didn't care who they were; I would have won. My fight was big.

*   *   *

Like before, I tried to look busy pretending to read a magazine. My frustration and anxiety mounted. Every time the door opened, I waited to hear my name. There was a weird sense of relief when it wasn't. Eventually, it would be my turn, and I wanted to get it over with.

My emotions rose and fell like a Mack truck over speed bumps. Even though I had been sleeping better with my CPAP machine, sleeping soundly during the trial was impossible, except once.

Each day I was subpoenaed to show up at court, I was given a window of four to six hours. I went through the formalities of checking in, walking into the little room, sitting, and waiting. Typically, I would wait the four to six hours then return to work. The Headley staff had become accustomed to me being absent a few days a week. Different agents took care of customer concerns, and accounts were prioritized. Fortunately, everyone understood the difficulty of being a state's witness.

One particular day, immediately after I sat, the lawyers told me I wouldn't be needed. I plodded out to the truck, wary from stress and tired from restless nights. The parking lot had been crowded that morning, and I'd needed to park in the back lot, which felt like a different zip code. I clicked open the locks and slid into the driver's seat. The car was warm from the sun, and I allowed the heat of the interior air fill my lungs. Starting the engine, I thought, *Good, I can get my day started.* I closed my eyes for a moment to reflect on my schedule.

I glanced at a full tank of gas, took my hands off the wheel for a moment, and uttered, "Wow." I had six hours. The fullness of the parking lot had thinned; my truck sat isolated toward the back, next to a set of railroad tracks. The office thought I was sequestered. I had nowhere to go and no place to be. Turning on talk radio, I laid my truck seat back. Reaching into my gym bag, I pulled out some clothes already packed for my evening workout. I made a small pillow and took a four-hour vacation from reality. The trial disappeared; the boxes of soot faded away. I imagined I was floating on a raft, surrounded by blue skies, fish swimming around me. Drifting peacefully back and forth, rocking with the waves, feeling the warmth of a Caribbean breeze, I relaxed. With my emergency brake on, I slept for the best four hours of my life. No nightmares, no terrors, no worries. I was a kid skipping school, even though I was the principal.

I walked into work six hours later.

Somebody asked, "What happened?"

"Ah, they dismissed me."

"Oh, that stinks."

I nodded then turned on my heel and grinned ear to ear.

*　　*　　*

As the trial proceeded, I returned to the witness room a few more times, each time knowing that particular visit might be the one that calls for my testimony. One morning about three weeks into the third trial, just over three years after the fire, a paralegal leaned into the room and said, "All right, Scott, you'll be testifying in a few minutes. Follow me." She was holding a stack of legal papers and had a calm demeanor. To her, this was all no big deal. In contrast, my heart leapt, beating rapidly. I nodded; my feet felt like lead. We walked down a side hallway and turned to enter the space in front of the courtroom doors. It was a waiting room with chairs and filled with people.

"If you sit right here, the bailiff will find you and call you in," she said, pointing to a section of empty seats. "Are you okay?"

My throat felt dry when I answered. "Yup, I'll be fine."

"Great. I know you will be." She smiled; it looked like she gripped the files she had been holding a little tighter.

I picked a chair and faced the courtroom. This portion of the courthouse looked more like a lobby than the little room I had been sitting in. It had the same tacky chairs and tables, but I sat in full view of the windows, courtroom doors, and elevators. The space was open and people periodically wandered from one side of the foyer to the other.

In front of me were two heavy wooden doors with brass handles and a sign that read: "Court in Session. No Cell Phones. No Pictures." There were, however, cameras and microphones and journalists. With each passerby, I'd raise an eyebrow, wondering if he or she were linked to the trial.

Occasionally, clerks of court would approach me to say I might be the next one or two or three witnesses to take the stand. Their vagueness kept me off-balance and anxious. The elevator doors would bing, and somebody would step off. Was he from a media outlet? Was she an attorney or a paralegal? Was I being judged while I was waiting to enter the courtroom? It had been a long and stressful morning.

Eventually, the bailiff came out. "The state calls Scott Headley to the courtroom."

I had reached the pinnacle of the roller coaster. My stomach lurched. The bailiff was a female officer, wearing the same gold badge and green uniform as her colleagues in the little room. I paused and prayed to God, *Give me strength to get through this.* Standing up, I saw the double doors suddenly grow twenty feet. My palms began sweating as if I were running a marathon. I wiped them on my pants. She turned her head from the courtroom and gave me a gentle, encouraging smile. Television cameras were everywhere. The seats were full. Everybody turned and watched me. Oddly, I was scared but not intimidated.

The room's staging was different than I expected. I envisioned an episode of *Law & Order*: on the left with his shoulder to the jury, Leon Davis would be sitting in front of the judge next to his attorneys; the right side of the courtroom would house a long table for the prosecutors. Instead, the prosecutors, defendant, and his counselors sat perpendicular to the judge and the audience, their backs to the side wall, all facing the jury, far from the courtroom galley, and more importantly, Ivanna's father, who'd tried to attack Davis after the previous mistrial.

"Scott Headley," I had anticipated this moment for the last three years. I'm an avid fan of suspense thrillers. Like millions of Americans, I know court procedures according to novelists and film directors. But I was a neophyte in real-life crime dramas.

"Do you swear to tell the truth, the whole truth, and nothing but the truth?"

I waited for the statement to be finished. But there wasn't any more. I glanced toward heaven and added, "So help me God."

They flinched at my declaration of God's guidance. I walked slowly forward and thought, *What the fuck have they done?* Leon Davis sat close enough to the witness box that I could spit on him. I wanted to flee; it was overwhelming and the weirdest, most unnatural experience. I actually sat in the wooden booth. The railings. The spindles. The judge, dressed in a black pleated robe with a white collared shirt and barely visible colored tie, sat above me like a king on a throne. And I began a silent chant: "Do not make eye contact with Leon Davis."

I peeked at the jury. Eight women, six men. All were ready to scrutinize me. They glared, their eyes cutting through me like lasers. All my nightmares, all my angst, all my guilt of not being at the office when that monster walked in, weighed on me. I feared the jury would blame me, like I made this guy snap, like I had something to hide. It was crazy, but I felt like I was on trial.

Then anger replaced my nervousness. Somebody coughed and shifted in their seat. I could hear the unwrapping of a lozenge. I took a moment and settled myself, concentrating on the light-colored wood-paneled walls, the stack of boxes behind the lawyers' tables, the florescent lights overhead.

I'd seen enough movies where the guy on the stand looked like an idiot. I vowed not to make my company or myself look like a fool. Instead, I focused on justice for my colleagues.

The questioning began. The prosecutor asked me a series of intense, lengthy queries. He wore a tie and dark suit. He stood calmly in front of me while I gained composure. We had prepared for these questions, and I felt comfortable with my answers.

When the prosecutor finished with his questions, the defense attorney came to the front. He was going to be my enemy no matter if he were female, male, blue, green, human, or alien. From my television-viewing experience, I assumed he needed to be good at arguing. His objective would be to trip me up or agitate me so much I become frazzled and argumentative. His job was to discredit me. He attempted that.

I also assumed providing truthful answers takes away the combativeness. He asked me the same question five, six, seven different ways. I did feel frustrated, but instead of responding with weak answers, I began to address each analogous question my own way: "I've already answered that, sir," "I've already addressed that, sir." My voice was calm, soft but direct and clear. He would twist a noun or verb, and I'd ask him to repeat the question. Suddenly I felt a swell of confidence because I thought he was trying to prove me a liar, and guess what, buddy, I don't lie.

He asked one very basic question: "Do you remember Leon Davis?"

"No, I don't."

"Do you recognize this file here?"

"Yes, I do. It is a Headley Insurance file."

"Do you know this signature?"

"Yes, that's mine."

The file contained lots of insurance documents, endorsements, coverages, and things not applicable to the trial. The attorney's goal was to dance with the jury and really make it look like he was diligent in his efforts. When I saw the signature, I realized I personally wrote Leon Davis's policy, which is something I rarely do.

And the memory of Leon Davis poured in on me.

* * *

I recalled a younger man in the early 2000s when he asked Headley Insurance to provide automobile coverage. He was proud to the point of arrogant about his car, an older model SUV. I didn't recall the value, but what was unique about the transaction was that he had doubled the amount of equipment inside the vehicle than the standard blue-book price.

His stereo had aftermarket amplifiers, subwoofers, and headrest plasma screens, to name a few. It's common in the insurance industry to do an intensive, detailed inspection of a vehicle such as this in an effort to prevent any type of fraud or errors of omission and ensure proper coverage. Leon Davis did not have a difficult time bragging about his expensive toys in order for my company to insure it properly.

The attorney asked me if I remembered Leon Davis after our initial meeting.

"No. He was just somebody I helped."

"How many times did he visit your office after that?"

"I don't know."

"Did you know he visited your office on December 12?"

"No, I did not."

"Did you know he was there to reevaluate his policy?"

"No, I didn't."

"Would you call him a regular customer?"

"Yes."

"How could you consider him a regular customer if you don't remember him after the first visit?"

"You gave me the file, and I can see his receipts."

"So you do remember him as a regular customer."

"No."

"Then how do you know he was a regular customer?"

"I can see the receipts from the file in your hand," I repeated.

The attorney's mind tricks weren't working. The whole line of questioning came down to whether or not Davis was a regular customer. That Headley Insurance was the reason evil brought duct tape, a can of gasoline, a lighter, and a gun to the office on December 13, 2007. That, if there could be a logical explanation for why Davis snapped that day, he would be a free man.

The attorney continued to repeat his questions.

"How many times did Leon Davis visit your office?"

"I don't know."

"You just said he was a regular customer."

"Sir, I understand your question, and I can answer it. But out of respect for the judge, jury, and everyone else in the courtroom, could you ask the same question all five times right now so I can just give you one answer."

The defense attorney did not like my reply. He paced, cleared his throat, and adjusted his tie.

Early in my insurance career, lawyers made me nervous. They had degrees from fancy schools. They spoke a language all their own. I learned they don't know everything, and their big words didn't mean diddly. And this defense attorney seemed just like the others I'd met.

I proved my own point when he asked how much money in the till had been stolen.

"Eight hundred sixty dollars."

He waved his arms as if he were trying to land a plane.

"Oh, oh, oh," he said and pointed to a sheet of paper in his hand. "We have a problem!"

The room became silent. Everybody focused on his next statement.

"You said here," he continued, "in the police report, $800 cash was stated on the remittance report."

He swayed and lumbered around to the jury box. He paused and looked at every juror. They watched him, a magician about to reveal his trick.

"Yes, sir, I did."

"So we have a discrepancy of sixty dollars."

"No, sir, we don't."

"Then, Mr. Headley," he said while pointing a finger inches from my nose, "can you explain to the judge, jury, and everyone in the courtroom this difference of sixty dollars?"

"Yes, sir. You asked me how much money was stolen."

"Okay, okay, okay. But the remittance report shows there was only $800 that day. You haven't explained the difference of sixty dollars."

"Well, that's easy. The office always opens with sixty dollars in the drawer in case they need to make change for customers. Therefore, if all the money is gone, that equals $860. Eight hundred on the remittance report and sixty in the till."

He was so angry he actually turned to the judge and said, "I need space."

The judge smiled. "Let's take a break."

And they dismissed me as a witness. My employees were dead, and all this attorney cared about was sixty bucks. I would have paid any ransom to bring them back, let alone sixty dollars.

I climbed down from the witness stand and caught the eye of the stenographer. With a raise of an eyebrow, she told me everything I needed to know—I won the day—and exhaled a sigh of relief.

* * *

On February 15, 2011, thirty days after the trial began and more than seventy-five witnesses later, the judge sent the jurors to deliberate. I drove to the courthouse and waited outside the courtroom, in front of the two large doors, where I had been moments before my testimony.

Two attorneys assigned to me by Nationwide Insurance joined me. Throughout this ordeal, they'd shadowed me and the prosecuting attorneys. They'd followed every detail, silently, in the background for the entire three years and two months since the robbery and fire.

"The judge is calling everyone in," a reporter announced, and all sorts of people filed into the courtroom. I watched a bailiff hold the door open as reporters and spectators vied for seats in the galley; every seat looked taken.

The jury had deliberated for fewer than four hours.

I stood to enter, and I felt my pulse quicken, knowing the verdict would be read.

"Scott, you can go in, but there will probably be a civil trial, and it might be best you wait out here."

"What?"

"If the civil case goes to court . . .," she began.

"There's not going to be a civil case."

"We hope not. But it's better for you not to talk with the families."

Civil litigation. I had been warned about it. I had dedicated hours to prevent it. But nothing about the fire or the deaths of Julieta and Ivanna was Headley's fault. There was no way, in my mind, we were culpable.

*   *   *

The last of the audience walked into the courtroom, and I watched the bailiff close the doors. They looked as I remembered, light brown, heavily lacquered, and huge. The lawyer held up a hand to silence me. A news crew was relaying the video feed from the courtroom. The words were read by a female jury member. "We, the jury, find at fault to count one of the indictment, the defendant is guilty of first degree murder as charged in the indictment." [13] I didn't need to hear any more. I fell back into my chair and bowed my head in prayer. Tears of joy trickled from my eyes, dropping wet splotches on my khakis. I wanted to hug somebody.

I wish I could have heard the cheer in the courtroom, but the doors remained closed. I continued to wait while others hugged, smiled, and cried with relief.

In less than four hours, the jury found Davis guilty. But I waited outside. When the doors finally swung open, jubilation reflected off the faces I had seen on and off for months. I, too, hugged people. I smiled. I cried with relief. But my world had changed because of Davis, and the guilty verdict did not undo the hurt and pain I experienced: the dull ache in the back of my head, the ants crawling in the pit of my stomach did not magically disappear with the pounding of a gavel.

The courthouse buzzed. Reporters from a variety of news outlets stalked Ivanna's and Julieta's families. It was their moment. Justice for their loved ones.

My attorneys flanked me, and we slowly walked toward the elevators. I turned to face the emotional crowd then turned back with the bing of the opening doors.

A few weeks later, Judge Michael Hunter upheld much of the jury's sentence recommendations with one exception. While the jury suggested the death penalty for all three murders, Hunter's judgment ordered Davis to serve life in prison for Baby Michael's death. I was in the car, listening to the local news, detached from the courtroom, alone.

Davis was sentenced for robbery, arson, attempted murder of Gabriel Brooks, and use of a firearm while on probation. He was sentenced for three counts of first-degree murder—one for Ivanna, one for Julieta, and one for Baby Michael. Leon Davis had his day in court. Evil didn't win.

There was a "but" in my emotions. I still felt smothered by that wet baby blanket from the curb outside the burned-out Headley office during the prayer vigil thirty-eight months earlier. Guilty verdicts do not erase bad memories or remove my feelings of isolation. Justice prevailed, but I was still unable to remember the happiness Ivanna and Julieta brought to my life. And I still couldn't talk about it.

DOUBLING DOWN

After Davis had been found guilty and Rick Richards already had over eight inches worth of discovered materials for the suit brought by the estate of Baby Michael and the suit brought by Julieta's mother, a judge mercifully allowed them to be tried together, saving both time and expense. Had they not been under the same legal umbrella, I'm sure I would have cracked more than I already had.

The first lawsuit was not about negligence or culpability. It was about Baby Michael. Baby Michael was born prematurely and died three days later. His brief life was fraught with hardship. He suffered as his mother suffered.

During the initial days following the robbery and fire, workers' compensation claims were made on behalf of Ivanna and Julieta. Baby Michael survived three days following his unexpected delivery due to a workplace incident. Baby Michael's suit was filed via a loophole in the workplace compensation laws. While all my employees are provided with maximum workers' comp coverages, Baby Michael was not, but it was reasonable he should have been. Finally, in November 2012, Baby Michael's estate agreed to a settlement.

The second suit pinned my father, as landlord, and me, as employer, joint defendants. This one claimed the brutal attack could have been foreseen and should have been prevented. I had waded through blackened boxes and answered thousands of questions for Richards. I had been inundated with issues brought on by Leon Davis for well over five years. And what didn't help was my father. Through my lifetime, he had been my teacher, my mentor, but as things heated up, he adopted a different attitude than I did. I wanted to fight; he wanted to run. His fear of a second heart attack stressed him beyond belief.

He called me continually, asking me, begging me to make the lawsuit go away. That I would be the reason for his second heart attack, that I would have four deaths on my hands. It flabbergasted me.

I had learned from him reputation ruled. I would not allow Mr. Richards's lawsuit to soil my standing as a husband, father, and employer. My desire to fight and not scamper away pushed me. We were codefendants and opted to share representation. I would fight with him and pay any settlement.

Through this process, we hired a private attorney, Chris Foley, to keep an eye on both civil suits. Chris was someone we both knew and liked. The focus of his job would be to make sure the Nationwide attorneys were watching out for our best interests. There had been stories where attorneys took advantage of clients, and my dad and I wanted to ensure we wouldn't be included in those statistics. But in order to ensure we both had the full attention of our lawyer, it was important we met with Foley separately.

But Foley began billing me for my dad's consultations, which included lunch meetings and dinners out. My accounting department paid the invoices without reconciling it with me first. I became irate and refused to pay any more. Foley, a bigger, bulkier man than I, stomped into my office and demanded payment, refused to leave, and decided to play bully. "I'm here to get a check."

I had been sitting at my desk, which was to the left of the door but centered in the space. To the right, a dull black filing cabinet stood tucked into the corner. A wall calendar hung between the cabinet and the window. He stepped up to me, invading my space.

"I've already paid," I quipped, pushing my chair back, causing Foley to step toward the filing cabinet.

"Not yours, you haven't."

"I've overpaid. I'd like to see a refund." My dad's bills were far steeper than mine. I stepped forward again; he stepped farther into the corner.

"You've only paid your dad's bills. I'd like to get payment for yours."

"No, I've paid my bills." I reached into a pile of papers and laid one on the desk. "Here's an itemized list, and my father's bills are not my bills."

He continued to argue, and I noticed a two-inch-thick case file in his hands.

I opened my drawer and pulled out my eight-inch legal file and tossed it on the desk. The weight of the papers thumped as they fanned out across the surface. The agony of each request for information made the papers in it seem heavier.

"Let me ask you. Whose is bigger?" Every question and every answer that had been exchanged with Richards sat on my desk. Copies of each correspondence were diligently forwarded to Foley.

We stood, staring at each other. I did not back down.

"Well, I hope you have a good lawyer!" he shouted, implying he would sue me for my father's legal expenses. He huffed and finally stormed out of the building; my heart pounded, nearly jumping out of my chest.

* * *

I was still convinced the second lawsuit would go away and not end up in court. I was wrong. Richards served subpoenas for depositions for eight or ten Headley employees. The day my deposition arrived, Mr. Richards held out a hand, but I didn't offer him one in return. I just looked at him with hate-filled eyes. My Nationwide attorney, however, did not have the same feelings I had. They chatted about the weather and how one of them got a ticket on their way to work. They laughed together—as colleagues, as friends. My muscles tensed, and I flexed my fingers and arms. I was furious.

"Okay, can you state your name?"

Duh, I thought, before answering, "Scott Headley."

"How long have you been doing insurance?"

I must have had a bewildered look on my face.

"I'm just trying to get to know you, Scott."

I answered his questions. In the beginning, they were silly, irrelevant. I wanted a battle; I needed the fight. I did not want him "to get to know me." I wanted to walk out. As the interview progressed, so did the questions.

"Was your security system up to date?"

"Is it monitored?"

"Do you have an emergency evacuation plan?"

"Do your employees have emergency training?"

Yes, yes, yes, yes. We sat in the attorney's office for several hours. The fight I wanted wore me out. Once again, I asked myself, "Why didn't I know this would happen?"

The criminal and emotional aftermath of Leon Davis's crime spree left me undone. My relationship with my father had deteriorated. I've had to fight not one but two civil suits—one settling and the other ramping up—and now my own attorney, someone I once considered a friend, was threatening me. I was no longer raw; I felt skinned alive.

With the civil trial date scheduled for November 12, 2013, I met with the team of attorneys, paralegals, and aides hired by Nationwide the weekend before the first day of court. I didn't realize the magnitude of what was going on behind the scenes. When I walked into their offices in Orlando, I thought, *This is a pretty busy place for a Sunday morning.* Attorneys and paralegals scurried everywhere. One of them came running into the building quickly enough to tell me my truck was being towed in the parking garage.

We rushed out; my truck hung on a hook. The attorneys forgot to give me a parking pass for my windshield. Awkward, of course, but we got the truck down before the meetings began.

They led me into one room filled with at least fifty file boxes, the disposable ones, designed to hold legal files. I studied the room and thought, *For a really nice office, these guys are a bunch of slobs.* Someone opened up with a small hello and began to introduce my legal team. The hive of activity, the six-foot-high line of cardboard boxes were there for me.

They even flew in a jury expert to provide support and a criminal profiler, Gregg McCrary, a former FBI agent who worked on some high-profile cases. I had spent the last six years toiling away in mountains of mush and dust. Memories haunted me, kept me awake, and away from recalling the joy of having mentored Ivanna and Julieta. I now had a team of people willing to help me reclaim my happiness. I suddenly felt like a rock star.

We plunged through rehearsals, reviewing notes and newspaper articles. I reassured them I never spoke an untruth and there would be nothing I hid that Richards could uncover. They asked again, "We need to know if there's going to be an 'ah-ha' moment in court."

"No, there won't."

"Richards will claim you knew this would happen."

"How could I?"

"Is there anything you're hiding?"

After all the inquiries from Richards and the defense attorneys Andrew and Rachel Nolin, I was convinced my life was ripped apart and splayed open for the world to see.

"I. Don't. Lie," I said emphatically. *Emphatically*, the same word uttered by the paramedic that caused the criminal mistrial. I meant it, emphatically, spitting each word out like a dart. There was nothing left to hide.

"Let's review what happened," someone said.

We recalled the criminal trial. Why did I not recognize Leon Davis before?

It became distressing. My guilt for not arriving soon enough to save my friends. They pushed me to consider things I had played in my mind like a looped movie reel for six years.

Leon Davis was our customer. He liked his toys. He came to the office the day before the robbery. The girls would have done a detailed inspection of his car, and the notes would have been in the black slush that didn't survive the fire. His midsize four-door sedan.

Next we relived the crime scene. In December 2007, a news reel of a midsize four-door sedan played nonstop by the Polk County Sheriff's Office. I remembered the video. It showed Davis, now on death row for the slaying of the two BP clerks, attempt to break into a BP station in Lake Alfred. A grainy video feed showed a bulletproof window cracking when it was shot. Another camera captured Davis running through the service area outside. Then calmly, he walked back toward the store. Davis tried the doors again then turned to leave. The end of the video showed a midsize four-door sedan driving away. The voice over the video offered a large reward for information.

I remembered how the murders of those BP employees rattled our entire community. Ivanna and Julieta would have been watching television, the news, the repeated pleas for information about the person who shot two men in cold blood just a few miles away, the large man in a hooded sweatshirt, and the offer of a $12,000 cash reward. They could have recognized his car when he came into the office the day before the robbery and fire. They did an inspection on his car.

The fire was not a crime of passion. It was not a spontaneous act fueled by momentary zealous rage or designed to cover up a robbery for $860, although it was what the prosecutor implied. It was premeditated. Davis walked into some store and purchased duct tape, a lighter, and a gas tank. Davis drove to a gas station and filled the tank. Davis packed a gun into a bright-orange, soft-sided lunch box. He dressed up. He parked. He covered the cameras.

My mind continued to piece the events together. This was not a crime of passion. This was an execution. The girls could have realized Davis had committed the BP murders.

Overwhelmed, I quietly clasped my hands over my chest. I felt my fingers tingle, knowing the truth. Richards was wrong. He had gotten under my skin, and I now understood the facts: The girls realized Davis killed the men at the BP station. They had seen the video repeated on the television. They knew Davis well. Maybe they considered turning him in. Then Davis realized Ivanna and Julieta knew he killed those men. Davis robbed Headley for money and murdered Ivanna and Julieta to prevent them from talking to the police.

Why would *that* not come out at the criminal trial? Would it be allowed to come out at the civil trial? No. Davis was found guilty because of Ivanna's dying declaration. Leon Davis did this, and she thought she would die. That was the information the jury needed to know.

Ivanna's dying declaration established Davis's guilt at Headley. The crime scene investigators matched a bullet found at Headley to the scene in Lake Alfred. The prosecutors used Davis's guilty verdict to establish his guilt at BP by tracing the bullets backward. And indeed, on April 29, 2011, Davis was found guilty of the BP murders.

I voiced my thoughts to one of the attorneys who suggested, without verbal confirmation, the prosecutors only revealed what was necessary to ensure a conviction, not muddy the waters to risk letting Davis walk with more hearsay comments.

I studied the tiles in the ceiling, recalling the words Judge Hunter said: "The crime was cold, calculated, premeditated . . . especially heinous, atrocious, and cruel." [14] The trial was so challenging Hunter opted to step down from the bench rather than run again, citing the *Davis* case as his most difficult. [15]

Certainly, I was not the person to understand complex psychological issues. I could barely grapple with my own anxiety and depression. I couldn't begin to comprehend what makes someone commit such a vicious act. All I knew, at that moment, as a swell of relief washed through my body, was that I witnessed the carnage someone can leave in evil's wake.

*   *   *

When the civil trial finally began, I felt like an abused dog. I had been shredded by Davis, whipped by the Nolins, attacked by Foley, accosted by Richards. The first civil case was filed in May 2009; it settled thirty months later. The second suit, filed shortly after the first, continued for an additional eighteen months. For the last forty-two months, I had been forced by the courts to remain silent about the events of December 13, 2007.

Gag orders are also called protective orders. Whom they are protecting, I'm not quite sure. Clearly, I was not allowed to speak to the media, and the media was not allowed to speak to me. But instead of being protected, I was forced behind an iron curtain, isolated and walled off. My whole life became the fire and robbery; my health and well-being deteriorated while the courts were "taking care of me." Now, it was a relief to know there was a light at the end of the tunnel.

The civil case lasted two weeks. Like the previous trial, I was unable to watch the proceedings in the courtroom, even for the final arguments.

I sat in the little room with the padded seats with chrome arms, a small wooden table, and overhead industrial lighting.

My name was called. A bailiff positioned me in front of the tall wooden doors. I opened them and walked to the stand. It was similar to the one I sat in a year or so earlier. The judge sat above me. The jury box was filled with six men and women. Five watched—one scowled with a disposition that said, "I am not a nice person."

The bailiff swore me in, dismissing God before I added him back in. And just like that, the confrontation began.

"You and your father, you were partners at that time."

"No, sir, we weren't. I was the sole proprietor."

"You and your father were in business together."

"No, sir, we weren't at that time. I had purchased the business before the fire."

Richards pushed. I did not waiver.

"You were en route to the office in Lake Wales when Davis entered the building. Were you going to meet him?"

"No, sir. I was not en route, and I was not going to meet him."

"You were traveling from the Lakeland office to the Lake Wales office."

"No, sir, I was not."

In truth, I was home, on the couch with a spinning room, uncontrollable cough, and a fever.

Richards attempted to raise my emotions, rattle my cage. He implied over and over that I, Scott Headley, was the reason the girls died. As my attorneys correctly believed, Richards made me relive the incident.

I refused to flinch. I hurt everywhere; I wanted to run and hide. Instead, I took the tongue-lashing. I had riffled through mountains of old documents and inhaled the black smut and filth left on the mountains of documents Richards "needed." I stood my ground. I am not the reason Leon Davis is on death row.

This time, Leon Davis's family wasn't there. This time, the sheriff's deputies weren't there. This time, the case boiled down to the predictability of Leon Davis's actions. That Dad and I did nothing to stop it. If a child of degrading parents listens to their hype long enough, he may start to believe the bad things they say about him. I had listened to Richards's arguments long enough; I had started to believe them—that I really was to blame. But I wasn't, and on the stand, I would not give him the satisfaction of degrading me any longer.

The judge finally sent the jury to deliberate. Hours later, we filed into the courtroom. The jurors had sent a note to the judge. "There's a problem," the judge said as he refolded the note in his hand. "The jury is unable to reach a decision." My heart raced. The judge spoke again. "I'm going to give the jury some additional instructions and send them back for more debate."

I watched as the jury left the room. They filed out, one by one, slowly. I pushed my head into my hands and prayed and waited in silence; small beads of sweat moistened my palms. Again, after a few hours, the judge unfolded his paper and silently read the note. His face gave away nothing.

"It appears, ladies and gentlemen, the jury still can't reach a decision."

The attorneys for both sides huddled together. Soft rustling of papers and scribbling of pencils reverberated throughout the room. Some were pressing cell phone buttons and putting the phone to their ears.

"I will send the jury back to discuss the case with additional instructions. They must now reach a decision, or I will be forced to declare a mistrial."

My hands began to shake. Two criminal trials and now two weeks of a civil trial, and we might have to regurgitate all this up again? Suddenly time stopped. The sour fragrance of old carpet lifted to the air as I felt the hard, solid pew-like bench against my back. The courtroom's formality sat juxtaposed to its simple furnishings. The judge, the stenographer, and the bailiff acted like this was a typical day at the courthouse. And for them, it was. For me, it was a lengthening of the tunnel.

"Go home. I want to see everyone here at 8 a.m. tomorrow. The jury will have one last chance."

Sleep, which always seemed elusive for me, was not possible. I'm sure, in other parts of Polk County, people connected to this trial had trouble sleeping too. At eight the next morning, the jurors received further instructions. There were whispers everywhere. The attorneys for both sides had no clue what caused the hang-up. No one knew which side was up or which side was down.

I thought back to my time on the stand. The jurors listened politely. They paid close attention; some even took notes on yellow-lined notepads. I remembered the woman who exuded unpleasantness. I thought, *I bet she's the one.*

For a third time, the judge called everyone back into the courtroom. He sighed as he read the note, letting out a disappointing "ah" just before my stomach plummeted. He made the announcement, "Ladies and gentlemen, the jury is unable to reach a conclusion. I must declare a mistrial. Everyone's dismissed." He tapped his gavel. The jury turned and filed away. They walked out of the courtroom and onto the elevators. I sat stunned, my belly churning, my head whirling.

Suddenly, there was a great flurry. Lawyers and paralegals scampered to grab their things, and dressed in their courtroom finest, they sprinted toward the doors and out to the foyer.

Some took the stairs, some the elevators. I didn't know what was happening. My thoughts shifted from worry about a second trial to bewilderment. Members from both teams knew what a hung jury meant. In a civil trial, if settlement is agreeable to both parties, it shall be taken. A second trial will not be advantageous for either side. If possible, the legal teams are allowed to talk to the jury after the trial concludes to determine what happened during the debate. Therefore, the rush to catch a juror was on. Just like some turkey hunts, all the jurors managed to escape.

I drove home, my language as foul as my mood. I inched into my office and pulled out my file of civil documents. I slammed it on my desk and said out loud, "I guess you're sticking around a little longer." I wanted to take my arm and scatter the papers across the floor. I wanted to stomp on them and tear them to pieces. Instead, I worked like a zombie. The albatross that hung around my neck pulled tighter. Two trials, two times.

I picked up the phone a week later. "Hey, Will, how are you?"

"Scott, we just settled."

"What?" I set the pencil in my hand onto the desk, sitting up straighter as I clenched the phone in my hand.

"The case, we just settled."

"How is that even possible?" I feared my hopes would be raised as I questioned, "What are you talking about?"

Apparently, Richards, who tried to beat me into submission, kept working on the case. He looked high and low to find a juror. After searching social media, he found the head juror who spoke with him.

After the first five minutes of debate, five of the six-member jury decided my dad and I were not negligent and had no way of knowing Leon Davis would harm the girls.

After another eleven hours and fifty-five minutes, they were unable to convince one mean old lady to change her mind.

Richards didn't like his odds for a retrial and opted to settle for a small amount in addition to attorney's fees.

We had the release of liability; it was over. Over. In an instant. No fanfare, no parade. All that was needed was a signature—a little, itty bit of ink—and my nightmare was over.

Will drove the paperwork from his office in Gainesville to Lakeland. The hell we went through together created a bond, an amazing friendship. That night, we visited a local eatery and enjoyed a steak and a beer. On February 19, 2014, we talked about other things. It was finally over.

* * *

Dusk settled by the lake. Reds, oranges, and purples colored the winter sky as I placed the final log on the fire pit. No humidity, no albatross, no sleepless nights. I lit the match and watched the kindling spark to life. Leaning back on the Adirondack chair, I opened the eight-inch file. Pulling a page from the top, I crinkled it into a ball. Toss, score. The ink-filled legal page turned green before it broke apart.

I chewed a Nicaraguan cigar and cracked an ice-cold beer. I pulled a long sip. It went down slow and smooth. I breathed in and relaxed my shoulders, listening to the fire hiss and sizzle. Smoke billowed into the air. I scrunched another sheet and lobbed. Another score.

It had been six years. Six long-suffering years. I threw another ball into the fire and watched my nightmare drift away with the smell of mesquite.

* * *

If only my nightmares were as easy to burn as the court documents. My drinking continued. It was my drug of choice to help me fall asleep, to empty my mind. My wife should have left me; my children should have forgotten me. I wanted to wander my tortured path alone, but my heart wouldn't let me.

Instead, I parked my truck in the rain and gave a woman my umbrella while she waited for a bus during a downpour. As I reentered my vehicle, I glanced at my reflection, distorted by rivulets of rain. I tried, fleetingly, to remember who I was. What I saw was a victim. I needed to make a real change—for my wife and kids. For me.

Seven years after Leon Davis walked into the Lake Wales office with duct tape, gasoline, and a gun, I checked myself into rehab for both addiction and trauma. I did the work. I walked the steps, and I talked the talk. While others who arrived after me progressed or graduated, I stayed where I was—only sober.

One night, about six weeks into my residency, a small group of us visited a dark secluded beach. "Stand ten feet apart." The order came from our chaperon, a big man with a rough voice and even rougher demeanor. "Look at the water. Smell the salt air. Hear the waves."

I walked toward the edge of the surf and stared at the shadowy ocean. "Meditate," he commanded, as if meditation could be forced. There were no lights to be seen; this part of the beach left me with an eerie sense of desolation. Suddenly, a peculiar feeling came over me. I started sweating, my heart fluttering with palpitations. The vastness of the sea in front of me was overwhelming in the pitch blackness. I panicked, dropping to my knees, fearing a heart attack. I choked in air, unable to catch my breath. I tried to call for help, but no sound came from my silent screams. I was alone, awash with fear.

I focused on a pelican that flew then landed in the water just feet away. My breathing slowed, and I closed my eyes. I relaxed as calmness flooded my body. I felt, for the first time, my ego disappear. I had talked my whole life about God, but after the events of December 13, 2007, I wondered how joy and terror could coexist. Remembering the horrors Ivanna and Julieta suffered, I questioned my belief in God. A voice came to me; it whispered, "Free will." I suddenly understood its meaning. Free to marinate in my misery. Free to be beholden to my nightmares. Free to treat those I love the most the worst. "And free not to," the voice said.

While on my knees, I felt the tug of strings on my hands and feet, and I prayed like never before. *Take my addiction, my fear, my anxiety, and dump it into the deepest part of the ocean.* In that moment, I let go of the anger and desperation I held on to so tightly and entrusted them to God.

Time stopped. I stayed on my knees until somebody hollered my name above the sound of the surf. I stood; no one else was on the beach. They had gone to a pavilion a hundred feet away. I trudged through the soft sand knowing I had broken a rule—never leave the group.

"Hey, Scott, man, what happened out there?" the chaperone asked when I reached the platform.

He was not a man I wanted to cross. His tattoos warned danger as he looked at me. I thought I would be sent back to the beginning, to start all over again.

"Scott, you had a moment out there."

I nodded. A moment. That was what Jake and Brenda Johnson wanted when they harassed me at the bar, when they "needed" to know what happened to those sweet, nice women, and all I needed was a drink.

The next morning, Bosco, a man who'd been at the beach the night before, asked me what took place by the water. Sitting on the front porch of the dormitory-style facility, the floorboards damp from a passing storm, we slowly rocked on wicker chairs.

"For the first time in my life . . ." I couldn't continue. I brushed a small puddle off the banister. My experience on the sand seemed more a dream than reality. I feared putting what occurred into words. My chair creaked in the silence. "Bosco, for the first time in my life, I was in the presence of God."

"I don't know much about God," he said, continuing to look over the horizon. We sat in silence, rocking our chairs, watching the storm pass.

After a long while, he pointed to the clearing sky. "Look, a double rainbow. You know what's at the end of it, don't you? A pot of gold."

"You know what the Bible says about rainbows?"

"Nope, don't know much about the Bible, either."

"After the great Flood, God promised to never destroy the earth with water again."

"Well." Bosco smiled at me and tapped the arm of my chair. "I think today, my friend, he's doubling down."

*   *   *

I returned home shortly after my beach experience, no longer a casualty of my broken heart.

"Scott," my wife said as she gave me a massive hug. We held each other for the first time in years. "I was so glad you left."

The odd greeting startled me. When I left, I didn't know if my marriage would be waiting for me when I got back.

"You're still here."

"It's just, every time you went to sleep, I worried what demons you'd face. When you left, I slept. The house was quiet. I knew you were safe."

"You didn't miss me?"

"Well, not for the first two weeks, anyway."

"After that?"

"Yeah, after that I started to miss you."

"I'm better now," I told her.

"I can tell. Your cheeks are glowing," she said as she put them into her hands.

"I don't know what I'd do without you. I still have work to do," I added, referring to my rehab. We talked that night, not as roommates and business partners, but as husband and wife.

I did have more work to do. I participated in intensive outpatient care. I attended daily Alcoholics Anonymous meetings. I started to mentor teenagers with drug and alcohol problems. I bought some toys for my garage—two new four-wheelers painted in a shiny coat of red. It's an uphill battle, but it's one I intend to win and have some fun along the way.

NOTES

1. ABC Action News, "Testimony in Leon Davis Trial Turns Graphic," filmed January 2011, YouTube video, 2:02, posted January 19, 2011, https://www. youtube.com/watch?v=PLSbiNPM7xo.
2. Bill Bair, "Invader Burns 2 Women at Lake Wales Business," the *Ledger*, December 14, 2007, A1, https://news.google.com/newspapers?nid=rwEhk56x NqMC&dat=20071214&printsec=frontpage&hl=en.
3. Bill Bair, "Invader Burns 2 Women at Lake Wales Business," the *Ledger*, December 14, 2007, A1 and A8, https://news.google.com/newspapers? nid=rwEhk56xNqMC&dat=20071214&printsec=frontpage&hl=en.
4. Bill Bair, "Invader Burns 2 Women at Lake Wales Business," the *Ledger*, December 14, 2007, http://www.theledger.com/article/20071214/NEWS/ 712140419.
5. Bill Bair, "Hundreds Mourn Lake Wales Burn Victims," TheLedger.com, December 21, 2007, http://www.theledger.com/article/20071221/NEWS/ 712210433?p=all&tc=pgall&tc=ar.
6. April Hunt and Amy L. Edwards, "Polk Woman Set on Fire during Robbery Dies in Orlando Hospital," TheOrlandoSentinel.com, December 20, 2007, tp://articles.orlandosentinel.com/2007-12-20/news/afire20_1_ polk-county-yvonne-bustamante-lucianolov.
7. Bill Blair, "Police About Davis: 'I Hurt Somebody'," TheLedger.com, December 15, 2007, http://www.theledger.com/article/20071215/NEWS/ 712150434/0/search.
8. Suzie Schottelkotte, "Suspect Praised as 'Great' Worker," TheLedger.com, December 15, 2007, http://www.theledger.com/article/20071215/NEWS/ 712150437.
9. "A Blaze of Terror; Leon Davis Case Videos; Reward Offered," TheLedger. com, May 27, 2010, http://www.theledger.com/article/20100527/ MULTIMEDIA/100529803.

10. Merissa Green and Shoshana Walter, "Davis Is Suspect in Two Slayings, Sheriff Says," TheLedger.com, December 16, 2007, http://www.theledger. com/article/20071216/NEWS/712160441?tc=ar.

11. "A Blaze of Terror; Leon Davis Case Videos; Scott Headley Struggles for Answers," TheLedger.com, May 27, 2010, http://www.theledger.com/ article/20100527/MULTIMEDIA/100529803.

12. ABC Action News, "Victim's Family Attacks Davis After Judge Declares Mistrial," filmed October 28, 2010, YouTube video, 2:31, posted October 28, 2010, https://www.youtube.com/watch?v=_tHCSJ-Qong.

13. ABC Action News, "Jury: Leon Davis Guilty of Murder," filmed February 15, 2011, YouTube video, 2:05, posted February 15, 2011, https://www. youtube.com/watch?v=7tmXyJwLZsc.

14. Jason Geary, "Judge Sentences Leon Davis Jr. to Death," TheLedger.com, April 29, 2011, http://www.theledger.com/article/20110429/NEWS/ 110429306.

15. Jason Geary, "Circuit Judge Not Seeking Re-Election, Cites Stress from 'Murder Division'," TheLedger.com, January 18, 2012, http://www.theledger. com/article/20120118/NEWS/120119377?p=all&tc=pgall&tc=ar.

ACKNOWLEDGEMENTS

I would like to thank all my family and friends who stood by me during this difficult period in my life and never gave up on me. Thank you for all the people all over the country that kept me in their prayers and encouraged me. A special thank you is due to my son Joshua. I am so sorry you had to see and deal with the things you did while all along doing whatever you could to protect me. I love you and I am very proud of the man you have become.

--Scott

I'd like to acknowledge the many people who provided me with support throughout this project. I'll start with my husband, Bob, who always believes in me. Thank you to Matt and Justin, for putting up with me, and Kendall and Derek, who have allowed me be part of their lives. I'd like to also thank Daniel LeBoeuf for providing me with hours of writing and editing counsel and José Toledo for offering valuable feedback. I would be remiss if I did not thank Allen Tatem from Native Imagery for our fabulous cover design. And lastly, I would like to thank Scott for entrusting his story to me.

--Alison

Originally from West Virginia, Scott Headley moved to Florida
to pursue a career in the insurance industry. Scott attended
the University of West Virginia, Parkersburg and is the owner
and manager of Headley Insurance Agency in Polk County,
Florida. He is an outdoor enthusiast and advocate for drug
and alcohol awareness at a local juvenile detention center.

After graduating from Norwich University with an MA in Literature, Alison Nissen taught composition and literature on various college campuses around the country. Alison is the managing partner of Three Dog Tales Productions, a ghost writing company and is a member of Florida Writers Association Board of Directors.

Printed in the United States
By Bookmasters